STONEHENGE

THE SECRET OF THE SOLSTICE

TERENCE MEADEN

SOUVENIR PRESS

Parts of this book were first published in 1992 by
Souvenir Press Ltd, 43 Great Russell Street, London WC1B 3PA
under the title *The Stonehenge Solution*

This edition, retitled, with the text completely revised, updated and abridged, and with the addition of new text and illustrations,
first published 1997 by Souvenir Press Ltd, London WC1B 3PA
and simultaneously in Canada

ISBN 0 285 63375 9 (casebound)
ISBN 0 285 63364 3 (paperback)

Typeset by Wyvern 21 Ltd, Bristol

Printed in Great Britain by WBC Book Manufacturers Limited, Bridgend, Mid Glamorgan

Contents

List of Illustrations

COLOUR PLATES

BLACK AND WHITE ILLUSTRATIONS

TABLES

Author's Note

I am grateful to the publishers for giving me the opportunity to prepare an entirely revised and updated version of the book formerly known as *The Stonehenge Solution*.

Since that book was first published new information has come to light, fresh discoveries have been made and some of the ideas presented in the earlier book have been modified and reconsidered. The latest research supports the basic message of *The Stonehenge Solution* which centred on the rediscovery of the importance of an ancient agricultural fertility rite called 'The Marriage of the Gods'. The concepts behind the cult were fairly universal among early agricultural societies and its demonstration for Stonehenge has proved to be irrefutable. New evidence has been incorporated into the text, various points clarified, and some of the chapters shortened or amalgamated. The resulting book is so different from the original that it was felt appropriate to publish it under a new title.

The story of the beliefs of the Stonehenge People at the time of the summer solstice is compelling and dramatic: it involves the celebration of life in a way that everybody who is close to nature and appreciates the human condition can understand. I hope that in this book its message now rings out more strongly and vividly to reach an even wider audience.

As always, I acknowledge the steadfast encouragement of my wife and family, and the artistic contributions made by June Peel of Bradford-on-Avon for the sketches on pages 21, 24, 43 and 118, and Maureen Oliver of Westbury for the two Stonehenge paintings.

Terence Meaden
54 Frome Road
Bradford-on-Avon, Wiltshire
February 1997.

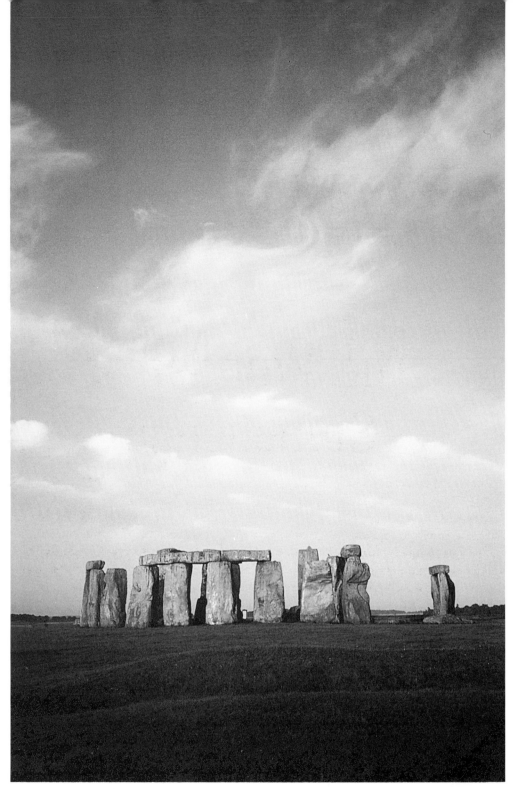

Stonehenge in ruins, forever appealing with its age-old secrets. Why was it built? How was it used?

1

The Wonder of
Stonehenge

The greatest riddle of Stonehenge is solved: why was it built?

Why did so much effort and devotion go into creating this megalithic masterpiece, with its everlasting aesthetic appeal, at a time when Britain was inhabited, so we used to be wrongly told, by tribes of battling warriors and primitive farmers?

The answer lies with religion.

This book sets out to examine the symbolism of Stonehenge and to derive the principles which directed its planning; it offers an explanation for the subtle ideas that led to the monument's unique blend of pleasing shapes and openings. These principles are simple and sublime: no mathematics, no physics, no computer modelling, no stellar observations—just the sun, the moon, and the common sense of human experience.

To understand Stonehenge we need to perceive the monument as its builders did, and to do that we must enter their state of mind. The archaeological evidence is sifted, the symbolism explored, and core ideas about the people's spiritual beliefs deduced; because, as with all feats of construction in prehistoric times, the compelling idea was a belief in the benevolence of fertility deities, and their promise of prosperity and a blissful afterlife.

The answers found for Stonehenge do not stand alone. Similar conclusions apply to the stones and circles at Avebury and elsewhere. For the experience of Stonehenge was but one aspect of the grand spiritual fabric of the age, repeated and adored universally—save that at Stonehenge the spectacle was given its most awesome and memorable expression.

It has mistakenly and pessimistically been said that we can never know the religion of those forgotten peoples. The ancient Britons left us nothing in writing, no sagas, no known traditions; their period of activity was so long before the beginnings of recorded history that it might seem that nothing of potential use has come down to us. Nonetheless, the clues are there, and as one searches, so they multiply. Marshalled together and sensitively interpreted, they present an impressive picture of devout, hard-working communities faithful to their all-powerful fertility deity who was a fully fecund, resplendent female figure: the Great Goddess.

The first constructions at Stonehenge went up in the Neolithic farming period about 3000 BC, but the spiritual story began tens of thousands of years earlier in other parts of the world, in the formative stage of spiritual thought when men and women puzzled over the origins of life and what their fate would be after death. Understanding key factors of their religion leads us into the British New Stone Age, where we find the chief ideas symbolised and interpreted in the timeless stone of a megalithic building era—in the stone circles, the chambered barrows and the megalithic carvings. But before then, in the fourth millennium BC, another kind of field monument had appeared. Astonishing for their immense lengths, these were the ditch-and-bank constructions called cursuses which ran for mile after mile through Britain's virgin forests and ancient fields. It is the solution to this little-known but substantial problem that leads to Stonehenge and the unravelling of its primary secrets.

Even in its ruined state on the windswept plain in the heart of Wiltshire, this finest achievement of the megalithic age is a majestic sight which attracts two thirds of a million visitors every year. Its ageless appeal stems partly from the very immensity of the stones, particularly the suspended lintels of the arches, but also from the circular symmetry of the anciently holy place, and from the eternal mystery that surrounds it.

Added to this is that singular charm which a monument acquires when its perfection is marred, a feeling of ambivalent goodwill as for a proud and elderly statesman suffering the degeneracy of old age. If only the builders of Stonehenge could see it now, they would marvel, too, not at the poignancy of the beautiful ruin, but because of the perpetual puzzlement it brings. Last century Ralph Waldo Emerson wrote:

> He builded better than he knew
> The conscious stone to beauty grew.

His words were meant for Rome, but they apply better to Stonehenge.

If we marvel at this abandoned ruin, how much greater must have been the wonder and fear that it inspired in the eyes of pious beholders and worshippers in those distant times; for they and their descendants revered the sanctuary for its profoundly spiritual values until its secrets vanished with the last of the peoples of the Late Bronze Age, around 1000 BC.

Then for three thousand years Stonehenge was silent, its worshippers gone, its purpose forgotten. The monument lay abandoned, crumbling before wind and weather, visited sporadically by the curious who could only stare and speculate as to why it was there.

'Upon no other subject, probably, have so many opinions been expressed, as upon Stonehenge,' declared the antiquarian Edward T. Stevens in 1882. Nothing has changed since. Opinions flow and ingenious hypotheses are advanced, but to no avail. This book, however, describes a breakthrough. The mists of time clear, and we peer—as if through an opening window—into the depths of prehistory. At long last important questions are answered and we begin to understand the monument's origins and purpose. That this has proved possible results from the new approach of seeking to uncover the elements of the religion and the basis of the spirituality which lay behind the design and motivated the immense labours of its construction.

The efforts of numerous predecessors were directed at astronomical matters. Sometimes alignments were found between stone and stone, or stone and horizon, or stone and star, which may or may not have been intended by the planners; but despite the variety of conclusions reached the theme was monotonous. Any alignments were assumed to be a primary inspiration for placing the stones in position. The stones themselves had no meaning. Any motivations other than astronomy were thought secondary, unimportant, or else beyond our understanding. This approach has been fatal, and has led too many theorists into declaring that we are never likely to know the true purpose of Stonehenge—or, for that matter, to decipher the majority of other outstanding monumental enigmas either.

I believe that it *is* possible to retreat in time, to think to some extent as our forebears did and, by uncovering some of the elements of the Neolithic religion, to re-create the basic ideas which inspired the planning of the monument. I have already described my findings in relation to circles, barrows, henges and megalithic art (see *The Goddess of the Stones*). In this book we concentrate on Stonehenge, Avebury, the cursuses and a few other monuments. What links them all is the discovery that in megalithic times neither a god nor a pantheon of gods was worshipped, but a goddess. She it was whose divine presence pervaded all nature—women, men, animals, earth and universe. At the beginning of the period which saw the birth of agriculture she was a fully fecund Great Goddess. There was then no Earth Mother in the agricultural sense; her rise, but only to a lesser power, came later, and on the way the Great Goddess became a tri-function deity linked to the cycle of the seasons.

First of all, however, we have to go farther back in time, to see whether the Palaeolithic origins of the Goddess religion can be found in the sculptured objects and rock

The distant Heel Stone seen through the middle archway on midsummer morning. The monument and its approach avenue are aligned on the point of sunrise for the second half of the third millennium BC—not on the Heel Stone, a solitary megalith slightly off-axis and just outside the monument. If the Heel Stone did not mark the sunrise position, what purpose did it serve?

carvings from those far-off pre-agricultural days. The heritage of the Goddess was truly ancient, for her cult came to Britain following 20,000 years of continental Palaeolithic prehistory, eventually reaching the British Neolithic Age with its barrows and cursus earthworks, its chambered tombs, and its earthen, timber and megalithic circles.

Trying to understand these constructions has presented endless problems. None of the monuments are what they seem. Outwardly, all we see are banks of earth stretching alongside straight or circular ditches. The circular types are called causewayed enclosures, henges, earthen circles, and round barrows, depending on their individual characteristics, place and age. The straight-sided monuments are mortuary enclosures, long barrows, and cursuses. Excavations produce pottery, artefacts, tools, and bones. Grave goods give clues about unknown religious customs. There are isolated standing stones and stone rows and avenues. There are rings of stone and rings of timber, stone cairns and stone houses, long houses and round houses. The monuments are numerous: nearly a thousand stone circles, forty thousand round barrows and cairns. The grave goods are studied, the clues multiply. But all the time most observers are not observing well enough.

Because so many sites contain bones, they have been called burial chambers or mortuary circles—mistakenly seen as abodes of the dead instead of temples for the living. Stone circles become dismal sites for ceremonial funerals instead of quiet or festive places for fertility cults, which they are more likely to be. Silbury is regarded as the tomb of a king instead of a seasonal centre cared for by a female divinity. Megalithic inscriptions are dismissed as having been carved without underlying logic, so that the spirals, zigzags, cup-marks and lozenges of Ireland and Britain have too often been regarded as ornamentation for art's sake. Megalithic yards and precocious geometers have entered the arena. The ancient world has been overturned, obscured, by a surfeit of modern knowledge and an uncomprehending viewpoint. This blindness was foreseen by the great Romanian historian of religions, Mircea Eliade, who said that to understand the lost religions we must enter the mind of the primitive. Admittedly, the dead and the living do sometimes come together in circles, on round hills, in chambered barrows, but they do so more for the sake and the future prosperity of the living—not solely for solemn burials and macabre ceremonials. Immortality aspirations and fertility needs were the compelling forces which moved the stones, not death and burial rites.

What building traditions existed at the time of the founding of the henge of Stonehenge when the circular bank was raised? In Britain around 3000 BC there were the causewayed enclosures, the chambered and earthen long barrows, the linear cursuses. There were wooden circles, but few if any stone circles. Ireland had 'passage-grave' temples, including magnificent Dowth, Knowth and Newgrange in the Boyne Valley, County Meath. Ireland's megalithic building era peaked before 3000 BC; Britain's would peak several hundred years later.

What did these peoples know that we do not, which impelled them to undertake public works on a scale so colossal that it was at the extreme limits of their primitive technology? The cause of our ignorance is the same as that which prevented other modern thinkers from grasping the solution to these ancient wonders: fifteen hundred years ago Christianity reached these islands, displacing religions which were themselves the degenerate successors to the megalithic Goddess religion—that much older faith which rose to glory in the period between 4000 and 1000 BC.

In megalithic times the female deity was all-powerful. *She* was the object of worship which drove men to move stones and mountains, to raise temples and shrines in her honour. She was the Great Goddess. As a product of Nature she symbolised Nature in all her aspects. Hers was the cycle of life by which living forms were born from the earth and went back to it at death to be born again. By the time the Christian missionaries arrived, she had long been supplanted as the primary deity. The Celts had substituted a pantheon dominated by male gods, but she survived in a form of Earth Mother under names such as Ana, Anu, Brigit, Brigid and Bride. The missionaries and converts could not immediately annihilate such a well-loved figure. Her places of worship and festive celebrations were Christianised: churches were raised in some henges and alongside standing stones; Christian symbols were carved on Goddess Stones; Eostre's spring festival became the Christian Easter, and the New Year festival of the winter solstice was chosen to mark Christ's Nativity. The Earth Mother lived on in popular belief, especially in rural areas, and fertility rituals continued to be practised by agricultural communities because Christianity could not give children to barren women or ensure easy labour as the old ways had seemingly done.

The dominance of the conquering religion closed men's minds. Men made the sacred laws and the secular laws. God-fearing antiquarians and archaeologists led the way in calling the prehistoric tribes of Britain and Ireland barbarians. Until recently prehistorians had no feeling for the spiritual sensitivities of those distant peoples, no wish to entertain the idea that Neolithic Britain lived largely in peace under the protection of a mother figure. Only now, in these newly liberal times, can we accept the evidence of the monuments for what it really tells us: that a Goddess was worshipped for thousands of years, that fertility practices were a normal part of life and that there was *never* anything in any sense obscene about them—as Hindus today would candidly affirm—for sexuality was regarded as the divine motivating power of the universe and its suppression was an autocratic decision of male Church leaders.

At last, without fear or shame, we can discuss the likely truths of the long-lost religion which involved tender and honest beliefs in the everlasting cycles of birth, life, death and rebirth. The early story of the Great Goddess will lead us to grasp the true significance of those ancient monuments which for so long amazed us.

2

The Universal Womb

Around ten thousand years ago, in the Neolithic era of Eastern Europe, the practice of cultivation began. The control and exploitation of cereal crops gave a measure of security to tribes who until then had relied for food on chance discoveries of seeds and fruits and occasional success in the hunt.

The seeds planted in the receptive earth passed through a cycle of growth, ripening and decay; for the first time humans played a part in regulating nature's life forces. The idea was born that the help of the deities had to be invoked because the agricultural cycle was part of the cosmic cycle which itself was integrated with the divine. Above all, the aid of the Great Goddess was sought, especially that part of her domain which was to become the province of the Earth Mother. With her help the risk of crop failure was minimised, the harvest made bountiful, the animals rendered fruitful. Without it, the seasons were irregular, the weather inclement, the routine endangered. And so it was that, in agrarian societies throughout the world, practical knowledge of developing farming techniques came to be supplemented by sacred rituals.

The Goddess was universal. Soil and earth were her body. Just as life issues forth at birth so is life reclaimed at death, for Earth is both womb and grave, at once fertile and protective. The reverence shown to the Earth by struggling farmers was due to Earth's inexhaustible productiveness; and the mystical link between soil fertility and woman's generative functions was the inescapable consequence.

Entering the grave, or going into a cave, was like returning to the womb. In Sumerian *matu* meant 'womb', 'underworld', and 'sacred cave' from the universal root for 'mother'—hence Latin and pre-Teutonic *mater*, and Old Teutonic *modar*. The relation between hole and ground or orifice and cliff was that of vulva and womb.

The cave was shelter and the cave was home—a haven from tempest, a place eminently suited to human birth. The same applied to the wigwam, the log hut, the stone house: they were artificial caves raised on the surface of the earth, the Goddess's body. Going home meant returning to the security of the Goddess's womb, a reassurance which made both life and death meaningful. The doorway was the vulva, chosen to face midwinter sunrise, so that it might admit and secure the rays of the New Year sun. The fixing of the solar alignments of various structures (tombs, temples, homes, and other buildings) was a widespread practice, but why were such things done? To understand we must enter into the mental universe of those deeply religious societies and discover the essence of their beliefs and ideals. Then, what appeared eccentric becomes regular, what was ugly becomes beautiful, what was inexplicable becomes coherent, and what some call obscene becomes proper. All this is relevant to the later Stonehenge story.

Whereas the Neolithic Age saw the ascendancy of the Earth Goddess within the Great Goddess's universe, fertility goddesses had been worshipped long before then. For thousands of years, in the Mesolithic and the Upper Palaeolithic eras, creator-fertility images dominated prehistoric sculptural art and rock engravings. Best known are the female statuettes of central Europe, which display the female form with exaggerated emphasis on the womanly features—the pregnant belly, the large buttocks, the heavy thighs. Vulvas and pubic triangles are often indicated, whereas breasts are less often amplified than 'modern' thinking might expect. This would imply that, apart from the primary desire for fertility, the sculptor's intention related to fears regarding the precariousness of the life-giving side of human birth. Such a statuette represented the fertile Great Goddess as she was to be viewed: the content of the Feminine at the time of easy pregnancy and safe delivery. It amounted to an appeal as to how she should function.

The so-called Venus de Laussel, a figure 43 cm (17 inches) high, was carved on the outer wall at the entrance of a cave or rock shelter in the Dordogne. Its date would be between 25000 and 20000 BC. There is a horn in the figure's right hand, with thirteen notches which may correspond to the thirteen months of the lunar calendar. In those remote times the horn may have served as a symbol related to the horned moon, and certainly it is true that the moon was very highly revered. The Moon Goddess was another side to the Great Goddess; in full view of the watching world she underwent a pregnant waxing and waning on a monthly cycle similar to the feminine menstrual cycle. Moon and woman were mystically united. The celestial divinity was Life-giver, caring for the female provider of childlife.

Such sculptures reveal a highly developed artistic sense, an achievement which could hardly have appeared 'overnight'. They would have been preceded by less well

Two of many female statuettes known from the Palaeolithic Age in Central Europe, *Left*: a Goddess carved in limestone from Willendorf, Austria, roughly dated to 25000–30000 BC. *Right*: a Goddess made of baked clay, from Dolni Vestonice, Moravia.

executed carvings, perhaps over vast periods of time. J. Munsch has recorded triangular pieces of flint from the Early Palaeolithic which had breasts and vulvas crudely sculpted on them by simple knapping (a photograph has been reproduced by Marija Gimbutas in *The Language of the Goddess*). Dating them by tool association suggests that they could be half a million years old. Not only is this vitally important as evidence of early artistic ability, but it proves how old ideas centred on Goddess worship might be.

Reverence for female fertility from those early times was also formalised by the carving of vulvas into the rocks of Aurignacian cave shelters. As Marija Gimbutas emphasises, the vulvas stood for the divinity, the essential part standing for the whole. The vulvar images of stone 'symbolise the vulva and womb of the goddess'. Archaeologists date the oldest of these engravings, by association, to 30000 BC or a little later. Examples can be seen in the caves of Abri Blanchard and La Ferrassie in the Vezère Valley not far from Les Eyzies in southern France. The vulvas, occasionaly reddened with ochre, signified the association of the caves with the womb of the Goddess. In a cave in the Spanish Pyrenees, at El Castillo, red-painted vulvas can be seen which date from the Early Magdalenian (around 15–17000 BC). In the same panel, painted black, is a flower or branched tree. Plant and vulvas share the symbolism of birth and growth. Besides colouring engraved vulvas in this fashion, entire niches and fissures in caves used in prehistoric times have been found painted in red ochre. This suggests that natural clefts and niches were seen as likenesses of the human vulva, which of course stressed their intended use as Goddess vulvas.

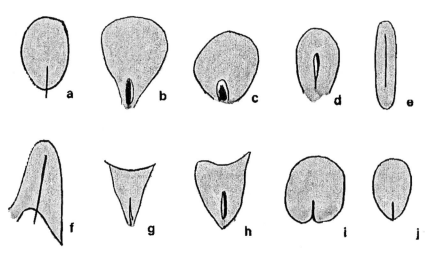

Vulvas engraved on rock surfaces in Upper Palaeolithic caves. (a), (b) and (c) Abri Blanchard; (d), (e) and (h) La Ferrassie; (f) El Castillo; (g) Pergouset; (i) Laussel; (j) Lalinde.

This painting on a cave wall at El Castillo, Santander, Northern Spain, shows five vulvas, each half-a-metre high, painted red. The plant-like feature is black.

Not surprisingly, any natural cleft in a cliff or split in a rock provided similar motivation for Goddess worship. Crevices attracted attention in all archaic societies, and have continued to do so right into our own century. A naturally-formed cleft in a rocky outcrop at Crawford Ranch, Canebrake Wash in San Diego county, was venerated by South California Indians as the Earth Mother's vulva. On the summit of the Wrekin in Shropshire is a cleft called the Needle's Eye. Folklore has it that girls squeezing through should not look back if they want to get married, and that their boyfriends should greet them with a kiss on the other side. These simple ideas hint at a deeper meaning born in an ancient fertility rite. Again the journal *Folklore* records that in the Highland region of Scotland, near Dingwall, there are two boulders in the Brahan Wood which lean against each other, meeting at the top. An old woman who died recently remembered that when she was a child she had a fit which her parents thought to be epileptic. So they took her to the leaning stones and lit a fire at the top, then passed her through the opening below.

It is the same with fissures in the ground. They attracted attention as Goddess symbols, eminently suitable as oracular openings and places of worship. In Greece

A natural cleft in a rock at Canebrake Wash in San Diego county, Southern California, an obvious site for Goddess worship.

the Delphi oracle was so named because not only did the word 'delphi' mean womb, but the site had a feature whose shape related to this. The same applied to standing stones which were naturally-fissured or artificially-grooved. The intensity of groove imagery can explain why Goddess-worshipping societies from Stonehenge to Orkney chose to decorate their pottery with multiple grooved lines, to such a degree that archaeologists call the pottery Grooved Ware and its makers the Grooved Ware people. It is likely that in addition to the spiral and the lozenge, which came to symbolise Goddess widely in the Neolithic Age, the groove also performed this function, whether incised on sacred megaliths, plaques, or pots.

Perforated stones, artificial or not, attracted similar attention from Neolithic farmers. The Bole Stone, Crouse (South-West Scotland), the Tolven Stone (Cornwall) and Men-an-Tol (also Cornwall) are among surviving holed stones in Britain, Ireland and France. Hundreds have been destroyed over the centuries. One, known as the Ring Stone, at the Avebury circles in Wiltshire, was eliminated only a few years before William Stukeley's first visit in 1719. The usual custom with holed stones was to crawl through the hole if it was big enough, or to pass children through, with the expectation of curing illnesses. Newborn infants were blessed in the same way. The symbolism is the *yoni*, the Goddess's vulva providing strength through the sympathetic shape of its immutable stone. Cures were expected because the rite related to rebirth. By the same token the Goddess Ring ended sterility. In Grampian a pierced stone, the Devil's Needle, remains in use today, where barren women used to crawl through the hole as a fertility rite, and still do so for luck.

Caves spell out vulva symbolism just as clearly. Their use through Palaeolithic times and into the Neolithic era meant more than just physical shelter from the elements; they provided sacred shelter from the dangerous outer world, for every cave was a sanctuary to the Goddess.

The crevice or cleft remains today a popular, well-recognised symbol for the vulva. Besides its universal recognition in the conch and the cowrie, and its everyday appearance in the indispensable grain of wheat, there is the popular gesture of the finger sign with thumb between index and middle fingers. This ancient sign was known to the Romans for coarseness and jollity rather than offensiveness. Since the complete message denotes conjugal union, in a prehistoric Goddess society such a sign would more likely have conveyed genuine goodwill, a salute for health and fertility at a time when these were the foremost desires of an innocent, peaceful rural population.

It is common, of course, for water to issue from natural holes, notably the pure water of springs or of underground streams. These were venerated throughout prehistory and well into recorded history, stemming from mankind's eternal need for water. Recognised as the source of life, the spring and well were held sacred to the Goddess who commanded their powers. Their reverence has continued into modern times, even surviving the prohibitions of Christian doctrines aimed at suppressing them. A tenth-century canon directed: 'We enjoin every priest . . . totally extinguish every heathenism; and forbid . . . well-worshippings, and the vain practices which are carried on with various spells'. Thus wells and springs, which are rather innocently regarded by most people in today's world, owe their continued attention to what began as Goddess beliefs in pre-Christian times, when the female principle was being honoured.

For tens of thousands of years, throughout which the highest respect was paid to the Life-giving Goddess, the vulva-cave was a retreat offering safety, a place for repose. This enormous time-span of committed reverence for a female divinity was devoid of any obvious signs of the genuine worship of a male deity. Male imagery does occasionally appear, but usually only in a subordinate or allied role denoting fertilising powers, rather than as an icon of some male god. Cave drawings have been found in Spain and France and clay phalluses in French Upper Palaeolithic caves at Laussel in the Dordogne and Tuc d'Audoubert, Ariège.

Caves with stalactites and stalagmites inspired a very special devotion from Palaeolithic and Neolithic races. Here the Goddess's life-waters could be seen in the process of *creating* life pillars of rock from the rock—phallic-like forms which became natural pillar shrines to the concentrated, regenerative life processes. Marija Gimbutas explains that subterranean crypts with a central pillar surrounded by offerings were commonplace in the Goddess-worshiping Minoan communities of the third and second millennia. In the temple-palace of Knossos, Crete, stone columns were marked with Goddess symbols of regeneration and rebirth, indicating that 'pillar crypts symbolised the womb of the Goddess Creatrix, where transformation from death to life took place and where initiation rites were performed. The participants returned to the womb—that is ''died''—and after the ceremonies were reborn again.' The pillar crypts of the early Christian Church unwittingly or deliberately took over this Goddess/womb symbolism—and then suppressed it, an idea that had begun more than twenty thousand years earlier with simple stalactite/stalagmite caves which were moist and humid like the human womb.

3

Womb, Tomb and Temple

Burial after death is the returning of the deceased to the care of the Goddess. In early times it was usual to curve the corpse in imitation of the foetal position. The desire was rebirth: like the planted seed which grows anew, a fresh beginning could be expected. In the Neolithic Age most burials were in long mounds or chambered tombs of earth and stone. Raising the mound created a womb, and sealing it interred the corpse within the Goddess's body. And as the chamber was the womb, so the entrance passage and door were vagina and vulva. T. Cyriax, in 1921, was perhaps the first archaeologist to remark on this:

> The earth under which men [and women] are buried is the mother of the dead. The object of the tomb builder would have been to make the tomb as much like the body of a Mother as he was able. The same idea seems to have been carried out in the internal arrangements of the passage grave, with the burial chambers and passage perhaps representing uterus and vagina.

Indeed, many of the chambered barrows were more than just womb-tombs; they were womb-temples, sacred places for rites and worship ruled by the Goddess.

In France a tradition of megalithic long-barrow building developed from the fifth

The Great Goddess represented by a vulva. This Goddess Stone is in a dolmen *coudée* at Luffang, near Crac'h, in Brittany.

millennium BC onwards, significantly earlier than in the British Isles. Goddess images with recognisable human features appeared on some of the big stones and this makes it easy for us to see them as Goddess Stones. Some of the other carvings whose abstract qualities made them less easy for non-specialists to recognise were clearly vulvas. The figure from Luffang, Crac'h, in the west of Brittany near Carnac, is one example. The expressive vulva epitomises the whole divinity.

At Gavrinis, an island off the west coast of Brittany, not far from Locmariaquer and Carnac, the walls of the great fourth-millennium temple-tomb seem to be covered in vulvas and, as a consequence, fertility symbolism. When this megalithic masterpiece was built it lay on a peninsula. Then, as now, it must have been an exciting place of pilgrimage for Goddess worshippers. Facing south-east, its façade is slightly crescent-shaped, and its aspect allows the midwinter rising sun to penetrate the dark interior of the monument through a low, vulvar entrance. Stooping, one follows the entrance passage for six metres, past heavily-carved orthostats lining the sides. The stones are of dark granite, a colour which evokes the darkness of the moist womb, for black was the colour of fertility in pre-Christian times (just as white was the colour of bone,

The Goddess temple on the island called Gavrinis, off the west coast of Brittany, contains the finest carved murals of Neolithic France. The long gallery and end-chamber are the womb-passage and womb of the Great Goddess. The decorated slabs are shown black. Only the quartz stone Q and the stones near the entrance are undecorated. Stones R8 and R9 are illustrated in this book.

and therefore of death). But the hard stone, an exacting medium in which to work using nothing more than simple hardstone tools, was elaborately carved. The curving lines which flow in multiple arcs and bands create an impression of movement and vitality as they sweep across nearly every stone of the gallery-passage and the inner womb-chamber. Yet the rising, repetitive, flowing arcs are not round circles, nor are they parts of spirals (although four complete spirals can be found among them all). As parts of elongated glistening circles, their effect is both surprising and mystifying. Why are they there? What did they mean? Whatever else, impressionable, free-thinking, intelligent observers have probably always had an intuition that somehow they touch upon the traditional mysteries of woman.

Now, as the secrets of the lost Goddess religion are progressively unravelled, they are easier to understand. Gavrinis *is* a temple to the Great Goddess, probably the most meaningful known site in France. Its images, architecturally and artistically, are those of woman triumphant in her life-giving powers. The panels are artistic vulvar represen-tations exalting the generative forces; labia, vagina, clitoris, are compellingly portrayed in the black, gleaming medium. The repetition of the motifs, panel after panel, reinforces the message. The Neolithic visitor, on following the passage and reaching the womb, must have been stunned by the power of the symbolism—as we are today once we understand it. For too long this place has been called a tomb although no bones were found in it. No, it never was a sepulchre; it was a place of worship, a temple, a shrine. Standing at the head of a peninsula, it faced the Atlantic Ocean which in some mythologies would have been the waters of the amniotic ocean. Marija Gimbutas was among the first to recognise the uterine nature of this great monument and to call it a tomb-womb and sanctuary, and I am calling it a womb-temple.

The first stone on the left on entering the chamber, C1, is important for its triple circular depressions reminiscent of cup-marks. In *The Goddess of the Stones* it is

Above: Vulvar symbolism artistically portrayed on stone R9 at Gavrinis. There is a primary central vulva with supplementary vulvas and multifold arcs to highlight their importance by magnifying the effect.

Right: On stone R8 the vulvas rise and multiply, reinforcing the fundamental message.

The great Goddess Stone inside La Table des Marchands at Locmariaquer in western Brittany. This enormous block is the terminal mural of an important Goddess shrine or temple. Centred about the half-metre long vulva is an array of Goddess hooks—every one an emblem of energy and regeneration.

explained how the triple cup-marks on the midsummer sunset stone at Newgrange represent the triple-function Goddess. Another stone, the seventh from the entrance along the right-hand side of the gallery, is of splendid white quartz. Although it is one of the few undecorated stones at Gavrinis it is a major Goddess Stone. Aubrey Burl has pointed out that the passage and entrance are angled so that this stone could be illuminated at the extreme southern rising of the moon, which happens every 18 years, as well as at the annual midwinter sunrise. The annual arrival of the midwinter sun is an important element, as at Newgrange. But why, and what did it mean?

Not far away, at Locmariaquer, is a megalithic monument known as La Table des Marchands, inside which is a mural which Marija Gimbutas correctly assigns to Goddess-vulva worship. Covering the huge triangular stone are rows of hooks or crooks, interpreted by symbologists as images of energy and regeneration, ranged on either side of a central vulvar-framed cup-mark sign. This cup-mark shows up well in oblique lighting and is easy to spot once pointed out. The repeated use of the crook-symbol in the design, together with the triangle, by suggesting the idea of pubic hair intensifies the message: that the tableau is a Goddess icon prepared for solemn veneration at a place of Goddess worship.

Two Goddess Stones with central vulvas from Knowth in County Meath, Ireland. *Left:* from a
stone in the western passage; *right:* a portable sandstone block, half a metre long.

Obvious vulvas appear too in the fourth-millennium megalithic art of Ireland. There
is one on orthostat 49 in the western passage of the twin-passage temple-tomb of
Knowth, and another in the vulvar design on a 50-cm long portable object, an engraved
piece of sandstone which George Eogan diffidently described as a 'baetyl'—a sacred
phallic stone.

The spiral is another Goddess image, particularly when left-handed, and carries its
own vulvar symbolism (see *The Goddess of the Stones*). The vulva also appears in
other abstract forms, notably as a lozenge or 'diamond' in the religious art of the Irish
Neolithic period, and in Anglesey and mainland Britain. Its use as a Goddess symbol
was widespread and continued into the Bronze Age period of Stonehenge: *as we shall
see in due course, there is a vulvar lozenge symbol on one of the stones of Stonehenge.*

In Britain a tradition of long-barrow building evolved later than in Brittany. British
long barrows date from the fourth millennium and continued in use well into the third
millennium. The word 'barrow', from the Old English *beorg*, means low hill. Long
barrows are frequently orientated in a generally eastward direction, mostly between
south-east and north-east. This indicates some mystical regard for the direction of the
rising sun, especially in connection with chambered long barrows. Of the non-solar-
orientated exceptions, the majority are earthen barrows on the chalk downs of Dorset

and the Stonehenge area of Wiltshire. By contrast, these exceptions form unique patterns of their own and are a vital ingredient of this book.

In the stonier areas of the British Isles and Brittany, long barrows and passage-graves often had stone-built central passages and one or more chambers. Because bones have been found in them they have usually been thought of as houses of the dead, but these barrows, too, resemble the womb of the Goddess, so they must surely have been built as temples to benefit the living. Excavation has shown that when the barrows came to be sealed in antiquity after centuries of use, some of them contained large numbers of skulls and bones but rarely complete skeletons, especially articulated skeletons. Corpse decomposition *in situ* leads to an articulated, ordered arrangement of bones. The finding of non-articulated bones indicates disturbance and rearrangement. Indeed many are usually missing, the long bones and skulls being most often found. This tells us something of the purpose behind barrow construction. The barrow takes on the air of a repository, a place where older bones get pushed aside to make room for later arrivals. Moreover, the later entries are not so much a complete corpse as a skeleton of bones which had been dried elsewhere, perhaps in a charnel house, before being brought into the barrow.

How can such a place be called a tomb when by its shape it seems to have been built as an extension of the womb of the Goddess? The construction plan of passage-graves and chambered barrows so often mimics female reproductive organs. Michael Dames offered examples from Neolithic Malta, and Marija Gimbutas found other examples from Neolithic Europe, ranging from Yugoslavia, Sicily and Sardinia to France, Ireland and Poland. Several shrines like this date from around 6000 BC. In

Plans of two shrines at Lepenski Vir, Yugoslavia. Marija Gimbutas pointed out that these are Goddess representations, the forecourt areas corresponding to the space between the Goddess's legs and the inner-space to her womb.

1924 the archaeologist Edward J. Burrow drew attention to the similarity of construction plans between the British long barrows at Uley and Stoney Littleton and the Maltese temple at Tarxien. 'Such a resemblance can hardly be accidental, and shows there to have been a definite architectural design for these prehistoric burial-mounds, probably associated with certain religious rites and formulae.' Edward Burrow saw the importance of similarity of shape; Michael Dames and T. Cyriax understood why.

In Britain, Ireland and Brittany many long barrows are clearly aligned on the midwinter rising sun, others less obviously so. A fine example is the Cotswold-Severn barrow at Stoney Littleton near Bath. The precise alignment of the gallery on midwinter sunrise originally went unnoticed, doubtless because the steepness of the hill causes a much delayed sunrise. This was no mere tomb to its builders; it was another womb-shaped temple.

Stoney Littleton lies between the Mendips and the Cotswolds, part of the fossil-bearing Jurassic belt that crosses England from Devon to eastern England. All the stones of the gallery and chambers of the barrow are oolitic slabs, obtained by splitting from a local outcrop or quarry. The barrow's stones abound with fossils, most notably *Gryphaea* (a kind of curled-up oyster known in folklore as the Devil's toe-nail), brachiopods, and ammonites well-known for their spiral-centred shells.

To judge by the strategic positions occupied by the stone slabs which bear the barrow's largest ammonite impressions, it seems obvious that these slabs were chosen and their positions decided by their petrified spirals. One of them, 20 centimetres in diameter, stands in the passage at the entrance to the first cell on the right. The other, technically the negative-cast of the creature, decorates the south-west door-jamb. The original diameter of this ammonite must have been close to 32 centimetres (13 inches).

In common with other chambered barrows of the Cotswold-Severn type, the stone-lined forecourt is curved into the shape of a pair of horns, gently evoking not only the imagery of bull-horns but the holy horns of the crescent moon. Moreover, the vagina-gallery is aligned exactly with the rising sun on midwinter's day. Every year for a few minutes the sun shines to the end of the long passage and a few moments later illuminates, on the right-hand side, part of a specially-selected stone which bears a deep, broad, natural cup-mark. It is not obvious from simple compass measurements that this is so. For a level horizon the sun rises close to 129 degrees from north, but because the barrow faces up a steep incline the sunrise is delayed until 138 degrees is reached. At that moment the sun bursts over the hilltop and shines brightly down the middle of the Goddess barrow, soon after which the cup-mark is reached. Why was it so important to get the sun's energy into the depth of the womb in this way, and at this season?

A second alignment concerns the ammonite spiral at the entrance to cell G. The full moon illuminates this fossil in midsummer at intervals of 18 years, when it rises at its most southerly azimuth of the Metonic cycle.

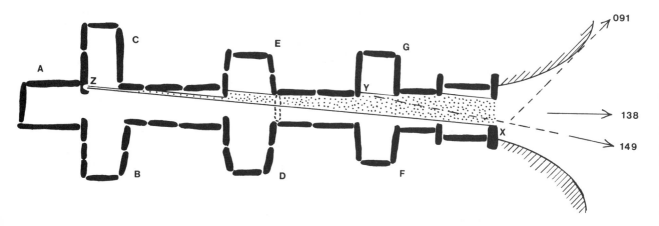

Plan of Stoney Littleton long barrow. The seven chambers are labelled A–G, following Arthur Bulleid. The vagina-gallery faces the midwinter sunrise (138 degrees from north) and allows a shaft of sunlight to illuminate the Goddess cup Z at the entrance to chamber C. X and Y mark the positions of prominent ammonite fossils. Fossil Y, which catches the midwinter sunshine annually, is so placed that it can only be illuminated by the moon at its extreme southerly rising (149 degrees from north).

Several symbolic aspects of the contemporary religion were designed into the architectural features of this unified Goddess-womb construction. There were the fossilised spirals of death and of rebirth, the mystic cup-mark (whose spiritual meaning is explored in *The Goddess of the Stones*), the curving forecourt, the alignment on the midwinter solstice, the extreme lunar alignment, and the fossil remains of petrified life-forms. The superabundance of life-death symbolism and Goddess womb symbolism indicates that the barrow was more than a place for the dead. It was a shrine for the living, and its cosmic alignments prove an intimate relationship between Sky and Earth at which the local Goddess awaits the annual return of the sun. One senses the presence of a rite which calls for the annual renewal of the world and its life-forms.

As at so many megalithic sites in Western Europe, Goddess symbolism forms the core of the constructional plan. At Lepenski Vir, the Irish court tombs and elsewhere Marija Gimbutas interpreted the forward extension of stone settings as the Goddess's open legs, and the crescent-shaped forecourts of the Severn-Cotswold barrows hint at this, too. This architectural trick appears at the long barrow sites known as Hetty Pegler's Tump, Notgrove and Nympsfield (all in Gloucestershire) besides Stoney Littleton. Long barrows in the Cotswold Hills at Cherington (Avening), Rodmarton and Nempnett Thrubwell in North Somerset (and probably too at Lanhill (Wiltshire) and Belas Knap) had port-holed megaliths in them which physically complement the

Looking from the depths of the womb of the Goddess at Stoney Littleton, showing the small area of sky into which the sun rises at its winter solstice. The position of the horizon is half-way up the entrance opening.

The constricted openings of some long barrows are plainly identifiable as the Goddess's womb opening. This sketch was made in 1809 by J. Burden in Avening, Gloucestershire, soon after the stone chambers of a barrow had been taken there following total excavation by the vicar. Leslie Grinsell suggests that the destroyed barrow was at Cherington a few kilometres away.

symbolism of the womb opening. The effect was produced by cutting half-circles in two adjacent slabs, except at Nempnett Thrubwell (now destroyed) where a single slab was perforated.

Lepenski Vir was clearly a shrine. So are they all. And many were temples too, functioning as churches of the Goddess, although receiving bones of the dead as did European Christian churches and cathedrals. The barrows facing the midwinter sunrise received the light of the New Year. Those facing east, as at West Kennet near Avebury, celebrated the equinoxes. Others, as at East Kennet, faced north-east—midsummer sunrise—as at Stonehenge. What spiritual reasoning drove the Neolithic peoples to create these alignments?

Timothy Darvill has summarised the radiocarbon dating evidence for the Cotswold-Severn chambered barrows. 'From the radiocarbon dates it is clear that the tombs were being built by about 3100 b.c. or about 3800 calendar years BC, and it can be suggested that a starting date even earlier would not be unreasonable.' The megalithic phase of the Wayland's Smithy barrow in West Oxfordshire has characteristics in common with the Stoney Littleton barrow, including fossil-bearing dry-stone walling imported a distance of 65 kilometres from the geological neighbourhood of Stoney Littleton. The single known radiocarbon date for Wayland's Smithy, indicating about 3500 BC (2800 ± 130 b.c.), comes from material which shortly antedated the chamber-ing of the barrow. Radiocarbon dating at the earthen long barrow at Nutbane (Hampshire) points to about 3400 BC (2730 ± 150 b.c.)

These dates confirm that for many centuries before the founding of the first Stonehenge (about 3000 BC), to say nothing of later Silbury Hill and Avebury, and at the time of the fourth-millennium BC causewayed enclosures like Windmill Hill and Robin Hood's Ball, a religion of the Great Goddess was prevalent and all-powerful.

Just how widespread was solar orientation of Stone Age Goddess monuments? A look at some supreme examples from other parts of Britain and Ireland will give an idea of its popularity.

On the island of Anglesey there is a round tumulus with stone-lined passage and internal chamber in which is located a free-standing megalith called the pillar stone. This is the famous Bryn Celli Dhu monument. The name 'pillar stone' was possibly selected by last century's excavators as a euphemism for 'baetyl' or phallus, but the stone is more likely to be a Goddess Stone. It seems likely that this megalith, as well as hundreds of others in Britain and Brittany which in a male-dominated world were looked upon as phallic, represented instead the integration of the sexes—that is, of the deities. In other words, in the symbolic reality of the time the stone stood for the generating power of the universe. As a holy megalith, it was at one and the same time a Goddess Stone, a life-force symbol, and perhaps pseudo-phallic as well. This menhir, like so many others, was a Goddess icon, a cult stone of the Age of the Goddess.

External view of Bryn Celli Dhu on the island of Anglesey. This Goddess temple has several design elements which demonstrate a strongly-developed belief in the world of the Goddess.

At Bryn Celli Dhu the slab-walled gallery pointed north-east, permitting internal illumination only about the time of midsummer sunrise. At this period of the year the energy of the sun would flood in, illuminating the chamber with direct and reflected light, although without direct light striking the Goddess Stone.

In the court cairn tombs of Ireland at Ballymarlagh, County Antrim, and at Deer Park, County Sligo, the passages with their Goddess 'legs' are open to the south-east; at Shanballyemond, County Tipperary, and Clady Haliday, County Tyrone, the direction is north-east, and at Ballyglass, County Mayo, it is north-west.

The religious imagery of the unrivalled temples of Newgrange and Knowth is explained in *The Goddess of the Stones*. The huge mound of Knowth is penetrated by two long gallery-passages, one from the east, the other from the west. At Newgrange the direction is south-east, and corresponds precisely with that of the rising

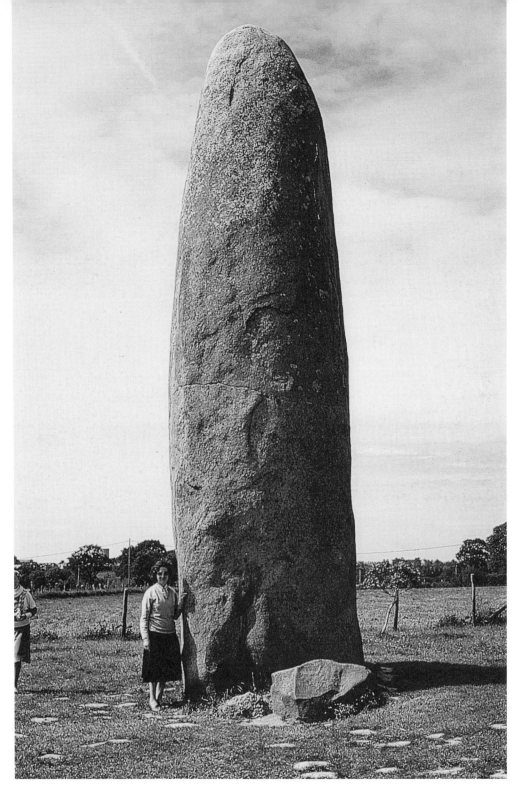

The splendid menhir at Dol, typical of the great standing stones of Brittany. Such stones were at the focus of a cult of the Goddess and some are carved with Goddess features or insignia.

midwinter sun. Megaliths stand outside the tumuli in line with the passages. Exactly what is the spiritual meaning of solar alignments? What mystical philosophy lay behind the physical reality of the sun radiating heat and light into the depths of a womb-temple?

4

The Marriage of the Gods

For thousands of years, during the Palaeolithic and Neolithic Ages, the Goddess was universally adored. She *was* the universe: Life-giver and Life-taker, source of luxuriance and fruitfulness, and the recipient of the dead who were born again from her womb. Many early creation myths start with a Universal Mother who generates by self-reproduction, or by marriage with a convenient god, a line of descent which leads ultimately to human beings on earth. Mircea Eliade held that the creation myth provided a model and justification for all human activities, besides standing as the archetype of a community's set of myths and rituals, and that every idea of renewal, or of beginning again, is traceable to the notion of 'birth' which, in its turn, goes back to the doctrine of the 'birth' of the cosmos.

A common element in creation myths and annual rituals, celebrating the renewal of the world was the Cosmic Marriage or Sacred Marriage—the union of the deities— which assured the everlasting process of creation and the continuance of the universe. Most obvious were the celestial marriages, those between the deities representing Heaven and Earth, or Sun and Moon. In Tahiti, as H. M. Westropp and C. S. Wake recorded in 1875, 'it was supposed that the sun and moon, which are gods, had begotten the stars, and the eclipses were the time of their copulation'. Mircea Eliade commented that the marriage of Heaven and Earth was 'often thought of in quite literal terms, *ut maritus supra feminam in coitione iacet, sic coelum supra terram.*' (As the husband lies above his wife in sexual union, so the sky covers the earth.) It is no coincidence that in European languages the sky is often masculine and earth feminine, the sun masculine and moon feminine. It is of course dangerous to generalise, for in some pre-Christian and pre-Islamic cultures, as in Japan, the sun was a Goddess. In Celtic Britain the feminine sun was called Sol or Sul at the time that the Romans arrived, and rites were observed on hilltops overlooking springs. In the Roman city of *Aquae Sulis* (Bath), joint altars were raised with the Roman Goddess Minerva under the name Sul Minerva. One of Bath's hills is called Solsbury Hill, after the same Goddess.

Although by Celtic times the once mighty Neolithic Goddess had been relegated to the subordinate role of Earth Mother or Great Mother and was serving as a consort to a higher male god, the Irish and Welsh kings still ceremonially married the local Goddess. Miranda Green writes that the council members or elders of a tribe acted as governors for a divine figure or queen, who personified the Great Mother and presided over a matrilineal society. The King reigned, not in his own right, but because he was the consort of the Divine Woman.

This rite of Sacred Marriage as applied to Celtic or Iron Age royal weddings was a degenerate form of an ancient tradition, but it hints at the character of the underlying mythology even if we cannot recover precise details. For the many people working on the land the paramount need for fertile soil ensured that the old ideas persisted in agricultural societies for hundreds of years longer, and to a small extent survived the greatest onslaught of all, that of Christianising reform in the first millennium AD.

So what can we learn of the Ritual Marriage in its formative days, thousands of years before the Anglo-Saxon period? The answers exist, engraved on cave walls, rocks and megaliths waiting to be deciphered, and they live on in the construction of the monuments, too. It is a matter of seeking the clues and establishing their meanings. If we look back at the Upper Palaeolithic period and then the Neolithic megalithic period, we shall find time and time again the plainest evidence of the Sacred Marriage myth, the Marriage of the Gods.

One image was found carved on reindeer bone at Laugerie Basse in the Dordogne, except that the male is not human. This telling picture, dating from the middle Magdalenian period, around 12000 BC, has been ill understood. Alexander Marschak has come nearest to providing an acceptable explanation. The legs and penis of a bull bison are seen high above a pregnant woman lying on her back, and Marschak suggests that the scene formed part of a ritual in which a woman and an animal told a story about the Goddess and a mythical animal, symbolic of the life-renewing force and perhaps intended to ensure human fertility, earth fertility or an abundance of hunting animals. What is more probable is that the virile bison is an animal manifestation of some

Carving on reindeer bone, about 15,000 years old, from Laugerie Basse in the Dordogne. It is likely that the carving represents the Divine Marriage between the Great Goddess and her God.

male god, a consort for the Goddess, whose phallic power arrives from above as if from the heavens or the clouds. In other words, the scene portrays the active relationship between the fertile deities, a form of Sacred Marriage, and is a plea for fruitfulness at the human level. Cut on bone the image was portable, hand-size; it could be clasped by a woman in childbirth.

An even earlier representation of the joining of male and female principles appears in a simple engraving from Isturitz in the French Pyrenees. Penis and vulva come together in union: a harmonious blend of the life-giving principles in partnership, the earliest known rendering of what may be the Sacred Marriage. Its age is judged to

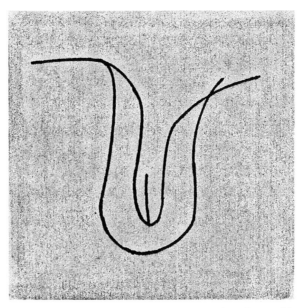

Penis and vulva in union—the simplest possible portrayal of the Divine Marriage or Sacred
Marriage theme. Stone engraving from Isturitz in the French Pyrenees.

be 21000–20000 BC. The deities are reduced to their essential attributes, which leads
to an extraordinary simplicity and economy of design.

During the long epoch of cave painting and statuary sculpture in central and southern
Europe, much of Britain and Ireland was under ice and uninhabited. Not until the
Mesolithic Age did hunters cross the land bridge from the Continent into Britain, and
then around 8000 BC the bridge was ruptured as rising sea levels created the Straits
of Dover. On the Continent, in the course of time, the agricultural age arrived and
the long-established Palaeolithic Goddess became the Neolithic Goddess. A major
centre of the agrarian revolution was Anatolia, now Turkey, from the heart of which,
at Catal Hüyük, comes one of the earliest recognisable renderings between human
likenesses of what appears to be the Sacred Marriage. The date is about 5750 BC. It
is a sculpture in relief with four images, which the excavator James Mellaart described
as two deities embracing and, on their right, a mother with a child. Mellaart wondered
whether these scenes might portray consecutive events: sexual union followed by the
successful delivery of a son. He commented: 'The Goddess remains the same, the
male appears either as husband or son. This may be one of the earliest representations
of the *hieros gamos*, the Sacred Marriage.'

All the concepts of the Goddess religion would have been carried into Britain by

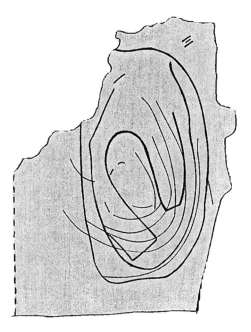

Drawing found on the subterranean wall of a chalk ditch at Dorchester in 1987. The theme is again that of the Sacred Marriage of the Gods.

the migrating hunters. Later, in the fifth millennium BC, the first agriculturalists would have arrived not only with their planting and husbandry techniques, but with an agrarian version of the Neolithic Goddess and her myths and symbols. A fourth-millennium occupation site and ritual centre in Dorset contains the oldest known mural in England: an outline drawing scratched into the side of a chalk-cut trench on the outskirts of the county town of Dorchester, the design restating the message from Isturitz. Sublime in its simplicity, it focuses on the essential function of the Sacred Marriage—consummation. It confirms that in Southern Britain around 3500 BC the ritual impregnation of the Goddess was already an essential part of the spiritual fabric of the dawning megalithic age.

Long before this mural was discovered in 1987 I had arrived at this conclusion, principally by deciphering 'the language of the megaliths'. There are numerous Irish and British megaliths and rock carvings of the fourth and third millennia which abound in cryptic engravings—spirals, lozenges, zigzags. They provide a symbolic legacy of religious ideas from the past which are a challenge to our curiosity. The symbols are not the random jottings of an idle peasantry but the deliberate carvings of a pious people and ruling priest-class. Left-handed spirals generally denote femininity and

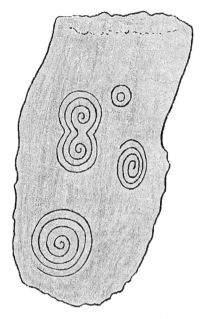

Megalithic engravings showing separate left-hand and right-hand Goddess and Sky God spirals and also a pair of opposites joined in marriage. This example is from the Calderstones, Liverpool.

the Goddess; right-handed spirals stand for masculinity and a male deity or consort. Outward-flowing spirals equate with birth, growth and rebirth; inward-flowing spirals designate death and destruction. Once we know this, and the meanings of lozenges, triangles, zigzags, circles and cups, we can understand simple stories and statements about lunar and solar movements which are engraved on specific stones. The theme of Sacred Marriage recurs frequently in messages stored for thousands of years, their meaning concealed until now.

The joining of unlike spirals produces a scroll-like coil, as at the Calderstones, Liverpool. It is found on door lintels, rock carvings, and standing stones. In it we see a Holy Marriage of the Goddess whose consummation guarantees the fertility of the Earth. It is an artistic statement of the life-generating union of sexual opposites which, by their marriage, keeps the divine cycle in motion. The symbol can be seen on stones and rocks which were carved in Britain and Ireland in the fourth and third millennia BC, and throughout the Neolithic stages of all the other continents of the world. In other religions at other times various images were conjured up to symbolise these same ideas. In Egypt the '*sma* amulet' was a sexual union design which incorporated the essential elements of the Divine Marriage. In Hindu India the Tantric altar-stone performed the same function for the primary deities. In China the Yang and the Yin featured a similar concept concerning the natural union of opposites. And in Western Europe the Neolithic mace, like the pestle and mortar, was a religious symbol of authority on account of its male-female integration within a Divine Marriage context.

There are several Neolithic megaliths in obviously holy places which bear the three-spiral design, such as Newgrange in Ireland, where all three spirals are left-handed, feminine spirals. The meaning is that of the tri-function Goddess. In other engravings, one or more of the three spirals are replaced by lozenges, so that the lozenge and the left-handed spiral both appear to be Goddess equivalents—emblems of august divinity. The lozenge shape, apparently—as well as other symbols mentioned in the previous chapter—is nothing but a representation of the Sacred Vulva. Its shape is not unlike the appearance of the labia at the time of giving birth. This quintessential female attribute identifies the lozenge as a symbol of the life-giving, child-bearing Goddess. In time it came to signify the Goddess herself, and must have been recognised throughout Britain and Ireland as her symbol. Being much easier to develop into design motifs than the coiling spiral, the lozenge became extremely popular, and appeared on metal and ceramic artefacts everywhere in Europe, including the Stonehenge region. Such a symbol is present too on one of the stones of Stonehenge.

A symbol which is fundamentally different in meaning but highly significant to an understanding of prehistoric culture is the circle. In Neolithic Britain this shape appeared everywhere in the form of stone circles, circular earthen-bank enclosures, henges, round barrows and round houses. At the stone-carving level it has been found as palm-size circles or cup-shaped depressions with or without concentric rings. Its chief significance was as sacred space marked out by the raising of a circular bank, or a ring of stones or timber, around a centre. The perimeter created, at least symbolically, a boundary between the sacred and the secular. The circle was the shape of the distant horizon, beyond which lay another world, chaotic, unknown and potentially unsafe, where strangers lived. On a smaller scale the sacred stone circle mirrored the cosmic circle, by enclosing an area of security where communication could take place with the divinity, as at Stonehenge.

In the middle was the Centre of the World, on the axis joining the centre of the subterranean world with the zenith of the sky. On ceremonial occasions the most holy object or person was at the centre, or close to it. In some stone circles a megalith had the place of honour, as in the middle and late periods of Stonehenge when the so-called Altar Stone stood practically at the circle centre.

All these sacred circles, whether of stone, wood or earth, were used for ceremonial and festive purposes. Burials took place at times, and rites and worship at these times and others. But there is also evidence of their use for happier, although still solemn, occasions, some of which related to fertility rites. The Age of Stonehenge came to be typified by the circle which appeared everywhere in monumental and round barrow

Feminine triangular and cup-mark symbolism as depicted on a British Neolithic cult object.
The sculptor has laboriously pecked a 50-mm deep cup-mark in the vulva position. The
triangular piece of sarsen weighs 31 kilograms.
The imagery reinforces the proposition that in the Neolithic agrarian world of Goddess belief
cup-marks on rocks and megaliths served as vulva openings for the passage of spirits.

designs, while the spiral and the feminine lozenge took pre-eminence as the cult symbols of the age.

As for the cup, this device was also related to the vulva and aimed largely in the direction of spirits. Proof that cup-mark symbolism explicitly stood for the vulva comes from examining cult objects from Neolithic Wiltshire in which the intellectual idea was put to use. Two sarsen objects with the shape of a pubic triangle are known, in which hemispherical cup-mark vulvas have been laboriously pecked into the hard stone at the appropriate position at the apex of the inverted triangle.

Thousands of cup-marks carved on stones or rocky outcrops are known for Britain. The cup allowed spirits to pass—those of the ancestors and those from the Goddess—and so permitted a degree of communication with the Goddess and the ancestors. Some cup-marks on standing stones were made to let 'fertilising' solar energy pass through, while others played a direct role in fertility rituals. The cup-and-ring marks, so common in Northern Britain, had a practical, highly specialised role—to release a spirit into the womb of a pregnant or barren woman in order to animate the baby prior to a safe delivery.

In the prehistoric world symbolism provided potent visual imagery to help the believer and worshipper understand the mythology and the religion of the tribe, and make sense of the mysteries of life, death and the universe. Such beliefs answered the chief questions raised by the early farmers: what were the origins of the seasons, of plant renewal, of animal and human birth? How could the resurrection of the world be assured—annually for the seasons, and after death for humanity? The Goddess religion must have provided satisfactory answers because it endured as a religion of comparative peace for the greater part of the prehistory of humankind, and this included the Age of Stonehenge.

5

The Sky God Mates with Earth

In all the surviving mythologies that have reached us from Stone Age societies there is a deep-rooted fascination with the origins of life and the universe. The myths explained and thereby validated—because they were held to be the absolute truth—the creation of the sun, the moon and the stars, the origins of animal and vegetable life, and the emergence of human ancestors. Just as importantly, tribal mythologies gave meaning to death by justifying people's beliefs in a paradise beyond the grave.

As the sacred history of the community, myths formed the basis of social life and culture, lying at the foundation of spiritual beliefs. Human psyche has changed but little since, although values and perceptions have, and later religions encountered similar problems in coming to terms with the genesis of life.

In the earliest stages of spiritual thought, from its beginnings in the Palaeolithic Age, religions were relatively simple, based on a supreme deity who in Europe was usually a Great Goddess but in certain regions and among some tribes in other continents was a divinity of indeterminate sex. In the Neolithic Age, as dependence on a farming economy developed, the power of the Earth Goddess grew within the domain of the Great Goddess; the concept of a union between Earth and Sky was universal, although initially the Sky God was altogether inferior in importance. The farmers of the Neolithic and Bronze Ages prayed to the Goddess and her male consorts to make the world fertile, joyful and intelligible, to bestow moderate weather conditions and a regularity in the changing seasons. And everywhere that farmers took their religion, symbol and image went too. Although people were illiterate, they knew how to express their main beliefs and prayers in pictorial code—on pots and on stones and rocks.

The realms of the Great Goddess were Moon, Heaven, Earth and Waters—she was an all-powerful divinity of fertility who incorporated the agrarian duties of Earth Mother. Only much later did an Earth Goddess separate out as a fully fecund deity around whom rather elaborate agricultural cults evolved, some of which filtered down into our own era. In the simpler myths of the Earlier Neolithic period the consort of the Great Goddess was the less dominant yet vigorously male Sky God, and in Britain there is evidence that he acquired a degree of importance quite early on—probably as early as the middle of the fourth millennium BC.

Wherever a Sky God was recognised, he was held responsible for the elements and vagaries of the cloud-bearing atmosphere. These natural phenomena are comprehensible to us because we have the benefit of scientific explanations and the wisdom of philosophical traditions, but in early times the agencies of nature were seen as terrible and awesome manifestations of the sacred. Above all else, the Sky God displayed his might in the thunderstorm, for which he was respected because of his prodigious powers of destruction and his ability to make the soil fruitful through his gifts of life-giving rain. Only later did he develop into a Storm God proper with his own highly developed cult.

As a Sky God he was the thrower of lightning-bolts and the slinger of hailstones. He announced himself with a thunderous voice likened to the roar of a bull; lightning illuminated the thunderhead and bolts shrieked to the ground, striking trees and animals and people. This was his terrible side; he was then the vengeance seeker, exacting punishment for some offence committed by the community, and occasionally called upon to bring destruction to the enemy. We know this through countless parallels from New Stone Age societies elsewhere, which provide overwhelming proof that from the time of Neolithic Asia and Europe onwards the thunderbolt, the axe and the bull were symbols closely connected with the atmospheric deities. Indeed, because of the much-studied religions of Eastern Europe we know how persistent these concepts were, and that they recognisably lasted through the Bronze and Iron Ages, through Mycenae and Crete, and into Classical Greece and Rome.

For stock-farmers the bull was the mightiest of the domesticated animals. They were keenly aware of his prodigious strength and of the instrument of his fertile potency. Consequently, because the thunderstorm sounded like a bull and behaved like one, the Sky God was personified as a bull or its image in the earthly rites of worship and sacrifice. At the same time the Goddess revealed her interest in the bull-cult through the horns which she displayed in her lunar manifestation. By their very

Bull's horns from a Neolithic Dorset monument. *Photo courtesy of the Dorset Natural History and Archaeological Society, Dorset County Museum, Dorchester*

shape bull's horns evoked the symbolism of the uterus, which has led Marija Gimbutas and others to suggest that the bull's head and horns displayed in a ritual context—known as the bucranium—came to stand for regeneration, representing the reproductive womb of the Goddess. Perhaps because they also created an opportunity to eat the meat, sacrificial cults and feasts evolved, and in later times, if not earlier, the head of a slain bull was offered to the celestial God and its blood to the terrestrial side of the Goddess. Remnants of ceremonial sacrifice within the prehistoric bull-cult survive to this day, for instance in the bull fights of Spain and southern France.

The cult of the bull became widespread early in the Mediterranean Neolithic period, and extended into the spiritual thought of the British Neolithic people, having been conveyed there at the time of the ancestral migrations which brought the first corn, pots and domesticated animals. Considerable evidence for the cult has been found from Neolithic and Bronze Age excavation sites, starting with foundation and funerary offerings in fourth-millennium ritual enclosures and long barrows. The rites included offerings of bulls' heads, at times with feet and other body parts of which only the white bones remain. A good example of a bucranium of *Bos primigenius* came from the infill of the fourth-millennium bank barrow inside Maiden Castle, and other big-horned skulls from Neolithic Dorset are now in the County Museum. The smaller *Bos longifrons* did not reach Britain until much later, at the time of the Beaker people.

There is another side to celestial potency, greater by far than any force that the ordinary thunderstorm can unleash. This is the tornadic whirlwind, which created such a wondrous yet alarming revelation as to imprint tribal tales with accounts that must have dominated mythological traditions for ever more.

The whirling winds of the tornado descend from the thunderstorm as a spinning funnel of cloud and roaring wind. For tense minutes the tornado pursues a straight or winding trail over hill and dale. Terrifying forces are unleashed. Everything is at risk: life, property, crops and trees. A swathe is cut through woods, a scar is left in fields; yet all the while the range of intense winds is localised, and a short distance beyond the limits of the path of devastation there is little or no damage. For the beholder it is awe-inspiring. An appendage like that of the strongest bull has swooped to the ground and made union with Earth. Witnesses liken the roar of a tornado to the noise of a thousand bulls—why not indeed? The tornado is the primordial Taurus, the Celestial Bull himself. In this role the Sky God has descended to the farmer's habitat; he has united with the Goddess, and track and traces remain as witnesses. The world of a Goddess-worshipping, agricultural community has seen Sky meet Earth. The community has been blessed with the majesty of a Cosmic Consummation.

To the Neolithic people it would be an act of creation, a Marriage of the Gods which maintains and revitalises the universe. The spiralling tornado funnel, sweeping field and forest in the thunderstorm, arrives at the peak of the storm. In hurried intromission a searing gash is cut across the countryside. But the climax passes, the roar recedes, and the air falls still. Spectators are dumbfounded. An event of cosmic significance has taken place on Earth, and been perceived as an act of sexual intercourse between the Bull God and the Goddess. The tornado track is testament to a Sacred Consummation between the divinities of Sky and Earth.

The theme of Sacred Marriage not only appears throughout the mythology of the ancient world, it continues into the well-documented classical period as well, and frequently alludes to intercourse between a Thunder God and Earth Goddess, at times noble and tender, at others raw and ravishing. This quotation is from the Greek Aeschylus who lived from 525 to 456 BC:

> The holy Heaven doth live to wed the ground,
> And Earth conceives a love of marriage,
> The rain that falls from husband Heaven
> Impregnates Earth; and she for mortal men gives birth
> To pastoral herbage and to Ceres' corn.

Another rendering declares 'the holy Sky is intoxicated with desire from penetrating the body of Earth'. Just as relevant is the union of Aeneas and Dido as told by Virgil (70–19 BC) in the *Aeneid*, for a storm erupts while the pair consummate their union. The epic relates that the nymphs are weeping on the heights of the mountains as the thunder crashes and the lightning flashes, signifying that the God of Heaven is approaching his marriage partner, the Earth Mother.

The myth of the 'creative storm' is universal throughout the post-Neolithic Indo-European period and every culture, which would have included the Age of Stonehenge

Two axe-wielding Storm Gods from the second millennium Indo-European era of the Middle East. *Left*: a Hittite God from Zinjirli; *right*: Baal from Ras Shamra, Ugarit. Because Baal has a lightning spear in his left hand, the Hittite God too is probably grasping a clutch of lightning bolts or their symbolic equivalent, which is an early version of the trident suggesting a male trinity.

too, had its weather divinity. The Storm God of the Hittites wields an axe in his right hand and holds an object representing lightning in his left. His long hair flows half-way down his back, ending in a spiral. The phallic shape of his cap may symbolise and augment his abilities to influence fertility. The axe-bearing storm god Baal from Ugarit, as portrayed on a relief from Ras Shamra, more powerfully features the pointed cap and spiralling hair, his most daunting tornadic features.

Another splendid representation of the Bull God or Storm God came from Jokha (ancient Umma, of Mesopotamia). The bull's horns, tail, erect penis and spiralling hair resulted in the figure of a commanding weather god, Lord of the Thunderstorm and the Tornado.

The Bull-God from Jokha in ancient Umma, Mesopotamia. The spiralling hair, horns and erect penis combine to create a formidable fertility god at a time when male gods were rising to prominence in the post-Goddess Indo-European era.

The pre-Iron Age inhabitants of the British islands have left us with no similar images of male deities (perhaps like the American Indians they fashioned their gods in perishable wood instead of immutable stone or ceramic) but these impressions from other cultures give some idea of how the British Neolithic people may have visualised their Sky God.

One clue we have closer to home is the British chalk carving, 55 metres tall, cut into the side of a steep hill at Cerne Abbas in Dorset. Although its origins are obscure, the style of its outline and emblems of fertility suggest a date no later than Romano-British, and it could have been cut and re-cut from an earlier figure dating from the first-millennium Iron Age. Despite being much later than the deities of the Neolithic era, it is a good example of divine masculine potency, shown as strength in arm and virility, the instinctive attributes of an agrarian society's god; clearly it descends in spirit from the beliefs of earlier ages. It may be no accident that this image is associated with a lozenge-shaped prehistoric earthwork within which maypole rituals were maintained for hundreds of years, and well into the present century—The Trendle or 'Frying Pan', or possibly 'dripping pan' as Paul Newman pointed out in *Gods and Graven Images*. He added that in country parlance the name alludes to the female sexual organ, which explains the name Frying Pan, the vulvar shape of the earthwork and the spring fertility rites held there. Similar reasoning might explain the name of the Neolithic spiral-causewayed site near Goodwood, Sussex, known as The Trundle. Folk memories can be long, and the origins of some names are thought to reach back to the Bronze Age and even the Neolithic. The belief that barren women would bear children after sleeping on the giant's penis could have originated from a desire for impregnation by the soul-spirit.

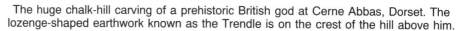

The huge chalk-hill carving of a prehistoric British god at Cerne Abbas, Dorset. The lozenge-shaped earthwork known as the Trendle is on the crest of the hill above him.

1. The Venus of Laussel the oldest known human sculpture carved to convey
a tangible message. She forms part of a Palaeolithic frieze at a cave entrance in southern
France. In her right hand she holds a cornucopia.

2. Swallowhead spring, whose waters feed the River Kennet, formerly known
locally as the Cunnit or Cunnt.

3. La Gran'mère du Castel, a splendid Goddess icon from Neolithic Guernsey. She has clearly
carved shoulders and breasts, and wears a necklace. *Photo June Peel*

4. Artistically portrayed vulvar symbolism on stone R9 in the Goddess temple at Gavrinis,
off the Breton coast. The power of the holy images is overwhelming and moving.

5. Stoney Littleton long barrow, near Bath, Somerset. Deep inside the passage the midwinter sun touches the cup-like pit of the slab in chamber C. Nowadays, an unplanned bulge in the gallery wall prevents full penetration of light.

6. Stoney Littleton. From inside the passage, the rising full moon is framed in the vulvar doorway. Its light strikes an ammonite fossil on a slab at the entrance to chamber G.

7. The phallus of the Storm God. A tornado funnel cloud over Hayling Island, Hampshire, on 27 October 1984. *Photo H.R. Lambie*

8. The Dorset Cursus, looking northwards across Bottlebush Down. The ploughed-out banks and ditches show up well, as does the Bottlebush crossbank. Along the centre-right a part of the original cursus bank survives.

9. The Greater Cursus, known as the Stonehenge Cursus, photographed from the air in 1987.

10. The sacred circles of Stonehenge seen from the air. The Heel Stone is at the top of the picture beside the main road.

11. The Midsummer Marriage. At sunrise, the sun's rays fall upon the Goddess Stone at the centre of Stonehenge. Three minutes later the shadow cast by the Heel Stone also traverses the broad, central trilithon arch of the outer ring of stones, and penetrates the inner sanctum of the monument.

Everything that descends from the heavens is sacred. This includes rain and hail-stones, especially when discharged from a thunderstorm, and above all the funnel cloud or spout. With its whirling, spiralling motion this is the supreme symbol of Heaven, for it is the only element of the atmosphere which returns skywards after descending from Heaven to Earth. The sublime fitness of the vision of withdrawal completes the celestial and divine imagery. The watching believer knows he has wit-nessed the penis of a god. The rain was semen, and lightning and hail were his arms and gifts.

What was the response of the community to this demonstration of celestial power? Interpreting the mating of the Sky God with the Goddess on Earth as an act of creation, their reaction was to prepare immense earthworks by which the area sanctified by celestial descent would be preserved as a permanent record of the tract of land where the divinities met. Today we call these exceptional monuments *cursuses*.

In his thesis on Neolithic cursuses Roy Loveday suggested that 'it is feasible that they were put up to demarcate a sacred area of land dedicated to the gods, a *temenos* or holy precinct'. This conclusion, although not specific as to its origins, tallies per-fectly with the findings discussed here.

More than fifty cursus monuments were constructed in Neolithic Britain. They con-sist of two widely spaced, parallel ditches and banks of very great length which ride the landscape, up and down, often for one or two kilometres and sometimes for much more. At least two cursuses are between 2.5 and 4 kilometres long, and the longest stretches for ten kilometres through the county of Dorset. Besides the spiritual purpose for which the banks were raised, they had a lesser practical objective. In order to keep such a vast area weedfree and treeless, the banks and ditches could retain animals for perpetual grazing.

As monuments go, most cursuses are hardly exciting to look at. After five thousand years little remains above ground level, and by the eighteenth and nineteenth centuries the banks and ditches of only three were sufficiently obvious to invite excavation, so confirming their discovery. Few people other than archaeologists and antiquarians visit even the best known cursuses, but these puzzling earthworks conceal some odd and extremely profound secrets.

The reason for their construction has been a mystery ever since the observant Wil-liam Stukeley, when walking near Stonehenge in August 1723, became aware of the importance of the 2700-metre length of parallel shallow ditches which pass from west to east less than a kilometre north of the famous monument. The ditches are about a hundred metres apart, the spoil from each thrown inwards to make banks of what were once white, but soon grass-covered, chalk rubble. Stukeley recognised the antiquity of these features and imaginatively proposed that the construction had formed a hippo-drome or running track which he called a *cursus*, designed for the 'games, feasts, exercises and sports' of the ancient 'holy days'.

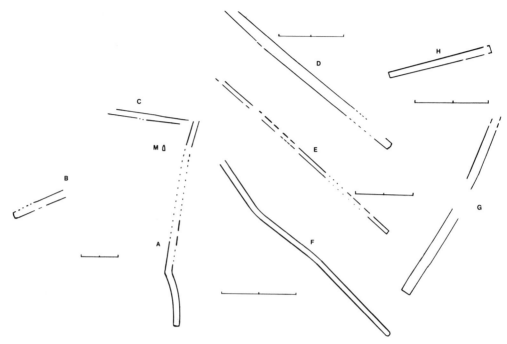

Eight of Britain's cursus monuments. The scales are drawn for 500 metres with subdivisions at 250 metres. On the left are Rudston A, Rudston B, and Rudston C in their correct positions relative to the Rudston Monolith M which is Britain's tallest standing stone at 7.8 metres. The other cursuses are (D) Dorchester-on-Thames (Oxfordshire), (E) Scorton (Yorkshire), (F) Fornham All Saints (Suffolk), (G) Drayton (Oxfordshire) and (H) Springfield (Essex).

William Stukeley's sketch of the Stonehenge Cursus with Stonehenge (E) visible to the south.

No full excavation has been undertaken of the Stonehenge Cursus. There have been exploratory digs with limited objectives, but additional probing and surveying have been made of the whole monument. It was found that the flat-bottomed ditches had been prepared by the laborious extraction of the subsurface solid chalk to a depth below turf level of 0.75 metres, and that the overall length, along both sides and including the high-banked terminal sections, was 5.5 kilometres. Man-power estimates by D.W.A. Startin suggest that a work-load of 100,000 man-hours was needed to complete the task.

At the base of the ditch section excavated by J. F. S. Stone was a fragment of Welsh Prescelly bluestone, about 90 millimetres across. This and other small clues from ditch and bank prove that the cursus was in use at the time when the pre-Beaker people were active at nearby Stonehenge. The ditches of the cursus had slowly silted up over the centuries, in contrast with the ditches of a possibly unfinished shorter cursus half-a-kilometre to the north, which had been deliberately filled in before time for silting had elapsed. The small cursus appears to have been abandoned in favour of building the second, although not before a series of antler horns and antler tools had been deposited along the ditch bottoms, an obviously deliberate act that must have had immense ritual significance. The partial excavations by Julian Richards indicate that both cursuses were constructed before the founding of Stonehenge (3000 BC).

The building of a cursus was a tremendous task for a simple society using primitive tools, but it makes sense if we see it *as the effusive devotion of an agrarian people for their deity*. The cursus was more than just a memorial to an exceptional event in their history because, besides marking the site of a Divine Marriage, it could be regarded as the Goddess's vulva. Either way it symbolised the Goddess herself. To plough the soil is to create a furrow, but to the devout believer every furrow became a vulva which took the seed and nurtured it. Seed-planting worked because of the influence of the Goddess on the furrow-vulva. Plough and spade were penises, and so was the tornado spout.

The majority of cursuses are one to two kilometres long although the lengths of several remain uncertain because the positions of one or both ends have not been located. Breadths generally range from forty to a hundred metres. This compares with the average path width of British tornadoes, ranging between 47 and 99 metres. Most tornado tracks are shorter than two kilometres, but at first glance many of the longer ones appear shorter than they really are, due to a 'skipping' effect (caused by intermittent ground contact), or to the tornado crossing open fields and leaving the locality altogether. For either reason, and perhaps to limit the amount of digging involved, the majority of cursus tracks, although tornado-derived, are under two kilometres in length.

Table I and the figure on p. 60 give comparative compass directions of 304 British tornado tracks and 26 cursuses. The tornado track directions were assembled using the data bank of the Tornado and Storm Research Organisation. The cursus directions were collated after studying the relevant archaeological papers and visiting sites. As the figure shows, the agreement between tornado and cursus directions is striking.

TABLE I

Tornado and cursus directions compared on an eight-point compass

TORNADO AZIMUTH DATA			CURSUS AZIMUTH DATA		
Azimuth	*Number*	*Per Cent*	*Azimuth*	*Number*	*Per Cent*
E, ESE	0	0	E, ESE	0	0
SE, SSE	5	2	SE, SSE	2	8
S, SSW	37	12	S, SSW	4	16
SW, WSW	140	46	SW, WSW	10	38
W, WNW	90	29.5	W, WNW	7	27
NW, NNW	29	9.5	NW, NNW	3	11
N, NNE	2	0.5	N, NNE	0	0
NE, ENE	2	0.5	NE, ENE	0	0

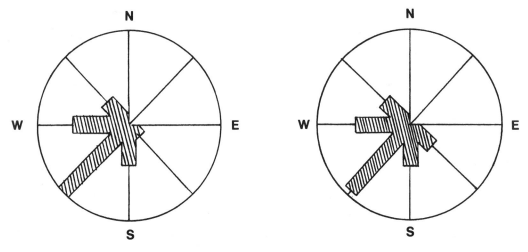

Direction comparisons between tornadoes (*left*) and cursuses (*right*). Most British tornadoes arrive from the south-west (46 per cent) and most cursuses are orientated south-west to north-east (38 per cent).

Although tornadoes are more common in Britain than is generally realised, at any one place they are a rare and unforgettable experience. The horror and astonishment that such an event brings even to a modern community are evident from contemporary accounts of a strong tornado which crossed a sparsely-populated part of Wiltshire near Avebury in the nineteenth century. The track dimensions, over a landscape of mixed arable and woodland, scale well with those of the Dorset Cursus, and the eye-witnesses expressed their feelings with a sincerity and humility that their Neolithic predecessors might have appreciated.

> In 1859, on December 30th, there occurred in Wiltshire, in the vicinity of Calne, an extraordinary tornado, as it was called, or one of those fearful storms which occasionally take place devastating a very narrow track of land, through which the storm cuts a way for itself, levelling trees and all other obstacles that oppose its progress, while the country on either side is left undisturbed. In this instance the length of country traversed was about six miles, the breadth being only 100 to 150 yards. The mighty rush of wind and all the consequent destruction occupied not more than five minutes. Amongst other effects a heavy four-wheeled wagon was taken up and carried completely over a high hedge, and straw and wheat ricks were borne completely away and distributed over the field never to be collected again . . . hundreds of persons came hundreds of miles to visit the district over which the storm had passed.

Three letters about this tornado whirlwind appeared in *The Times*. One said:

> It appeared to have been a regular tornado, having a curvilinear motion, and progressing at a regular rate. Symptoms of an approaching storm were visible at 1 o'clock p.m. The whole atmosphere became thick and heavy. It was so dark that it was scarcely possible to read without artificial light. Presently the vault of heaven was lit up by vivid flashes of lightning, accompanied by loud and sudden claps of thunder, which together with the big hail stones falling thick and fast, and the roaring of the mighty wind, produced a scene at once awful and sublime. The whirlwind seemed to commence on the outskirts of Bowood park . . .

The direction of the track was from west-south-west to east-north-east, the most frequent tornado direction and the one which happens to be the most common cursus orientation as well. The tornado pursued its path of devastation through the villages of Quemerford, Cherhill, and Yatesbury, a distance of ten kilometres. Beyond this the countryside is more open, for it constitutes the fertile agricultural land and rolling downs that are west, north and north-east of Avebury. Indeed, the tornado funnel must have passed close to the Neolithic causewayed enclosure on Windmill Hill, not far north of the ancient stone avenue west of Avebury. Particulars were given in the

Wiltshire Archaeological Magazine by the Rev. A. C. Smith, vicar of Yatesbury, whose rectory narrowly escaped harm. He recorded the severe building damage occasioned to Yatesbury and the distant village of Winterbourne Monkton and to isolated farms on Hackpen Hill and near Rockley.

The effect on a modern population, and on the writers, is notable. Describing the vision presented by the tornado the Rev. Mr Smith wrote:

> Several persons saw it from a short distance, coming up over the open down, but being on one side of its course, they were entirely out of it, and felt none of its breath as it tore by. Some of these witnesses describe it as a thick volume of smoke, or a dense cloud of steam rushing through the air: but to those within its line, so appalling was its appearance, and so terrific the roar of its approach, that the stoutest heart felt unnerved, and the steadiest head bewildered at so sudden, so unusual, and so fearful a visitation ... And so sudden and furious was its onset, so loud and deafening its roar, so strange and unearthly the darkness (not unlike that attending the annular eclipse of the sun the previous year), so terrific the crash of falling roofs (tiles and rafters and thatch seeming to fill the air, while the windows were beaten in by the hail), that many thought the Judgment Day had arrived, and others believed an earthquake was demolishing their homes.

The power of the elements impressed the observers of the nineteenth century even as it does today, for tornadoes are infrequent enough and strong enough to justify the attention they get. It is hardly surprising that an archaic community, with no explanation for such a storm, should have seen it as the advent of the Sky God who vaunted his powers while violating and impregnating Earth. So, all those centuries ago, in Neolithic Britain, the cursus was built to commemorate a tornado, that everyone might know of their closeness to the gods. The event would become part of the community's oral mythology, and the descendants would benefit by the cohesion of the group and exclusion of outsiders from knowledge of an historical act identifiable with the time of their ancestors.

Two other points regarding the Wiltshire tornado of 1859 are important. The first is the giant hail, a common accompaniment to great thunderstorms and tornadoes. As bodies cast out by the Storm God, hailstones would have a highly prized though short life. The fabrication of imitation hailstones in chalk, limestone and other rocks would provide exquisite accessories for the sacramental work of the priest or priestess, and may explain some of the rounded or spherically-shaped rocks whose prehistoric purpose has been regarded as a mystery or else ascribed largely to male fertility matters.

The second point is the date of this tornado, 30 December. It is a fact that British autumns and winters produce more tornadoes than springs and summers. Enthusiasm

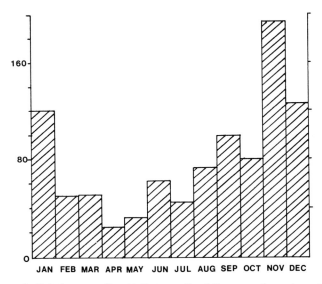

Tornado frequency in Britain according to the month of the year, based on data for the 35 years ending in 1984.

for cursus construction might be greatest and manpower more readily forthcoming at this low point of the agricultural year.

If the cursus builders wished to celebrate the anniversary of their cosmic visit, the most effective way of registering the date for all time would be to incorporate a sunrise or sunset alignment within the monument. This I believe was done for the Dorset Cursus. If it had been done for the Calne tornado, the commemoration date of 30 December would have given a sunrise direction not significantly different from that of the solstice. An alignment to indicate the time of day at which the tornado struck might also have been recorded, so that at the anniversary celebrations the time of occurrence, even perhaps its duration, could be precisely reconstituted.

Examples of strong tornadoes could be multiplied indefinitely. Historical accounts of more than 2,000 British tornadoes, dating back to the eleventh century, are held in the archives of the Tornado and Storm Research Organisation, Oxford Brookes University.

What are the characteristics of tornado tracks that make them appear so similar to the outlines of British cursus monuments?

Over level ground tornado tracks normally run in straight lines, or nearly so, and maintain this regularity across meadow and field, sometimes for kilometres, even over rivers and through forests, so long as the terrain remains comparatively flat. Occasionally the longer tracks curve gradually, turning slowly either to left or right, remarkably like the cursuses illustrated on p. 58.

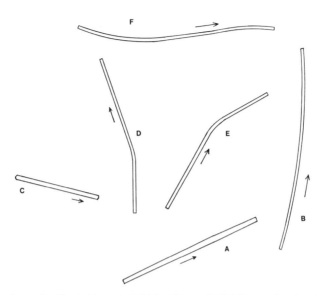

Six British tornado paths illustrating straight tracks and slightly-curving tracks (not drawn to scale). Two examples of kinked paths are included. Lengths vary between half and three kilometres. A: Sussex 1983; B: Berkshire 1979; C: Cambridgeshire 1981; D: Leicestershire 1982; E: Kent 1980; F: Lincolnshire 1982.

On the other hand, especially when travelling over undulating country, tornado tracks occasionally change direction more obviously, either abruptly or in a long sweeping bend, and sometimes this seems due to a change in the slope of the terrain.

Three other features of tornado tracks need mentioning. The first is a variation in breadth, where the track widens or narrows. This is found, too, in the cursuses at Springfield (Essex) and Fornham All Saints (Suffolk) among others, and is a well-known feature of the Stonehenge and the Dorset Cursuses. The second is a skipping effect in which a conspicuous obstruction, perhaps part of a farm or wood, escapes obvious damage due to a lifting of the foot of the twisting funnel above a part of the course. The tornado which is suggested as responsible for the Drayton cursus in Oxfordshire may have skipped in this way, if the gap in its path dates from Neolithic times. A third characteristic is a tendency for the track to follow a long, gentle arc—which surveyors would find vastly more difficult to engineer in the absence of the guiding curve of a tornado track than they would the already problematical feat of marking out a long straight line over hill and dale.

All the properties of tornado tracks described above have their parallels in the idiosyncrasies of the Neolithic cursuses, and the colossal Dorset Cursus includes most of them in the course of its great length. Stretching for 9.6 kilometres across Cranborne

Chase in northern Dorset, it was built in the Earlier Neolithic period, about the middle of the fourth millennium. Much of Britain was covered by dense woodland, broken only by islands of cultivation whose pattern shifted about as soils worsened and crop-yields fell, encouraging the farmers to attack fresh forest by, most likely, slash and burn methods.

Like all cursuses the Dorset Cursus is an elongated area enclosed by banks and external ditches. To complete the enclosure almost twenty kilometres of ditch were cut through the thin turf to a depth of nearly two metres in the subsoil chalk. The best estimate of the labour required is that of D. W. A. Startin, who arrived at 450,000 man-hours. This mighty feat of engineering was followed by an extensive programme of barrow-building. In all, sixteen long barrows were constructed close to the cursus. Two are out of sight of it and may already have been there before it was built. Of the remaining fourteen, two are inside the cursus and all of them, apart from their ritual and ceremonial functions, must surely have been planned and positioned to serve as directional indicators. This point is indisputable because of their inbuilt compass orientations.

The cursus starts on Thickthorn Down in the parish of Gussage St Michael, ten kilometres north-east of the town of Blandford Forum. The terminal is marked by a bank 80–100 metres in length, which is now 18 metres wide and two metres above

Aerial view of the terminal bank of the Dorset Cursus on Thickthorn Down. It is still in place after 5,500 years, but the cursus banks to its north have been obliterated. The long barrow on the right is Gussage St Michael I.

the present bottom of the much-silted outer ditch. This is impressive for a bank that was never more than an unsupported heap of earth and chalk rubble and which has resisted the action of time and weather for 5,500 years. Close to the south-east are two long mounds of long-barrow type (called Gussage St Michael I and II) which seem to be an important part of the terminal construction scheme.

From windswept Thickthorn Down the cursus descends east-north-eastwards, in the guise of a former pair of low banks and ditches around a hundred metres apart. The ditches have long since disappeared, filled by the ceaseless action of weathering and farming, although at certain seasons their locations are visible from the ground or air by anomalies in vegetation growth. The cursus turns slightly and after a kilometre traverses watermeadows and a brook by Higher Farm. It is worth noting that neither a racecourse nor a ceremonial way would from choice be directed into swampy meadows and across a stream, whereas any insensitive 'divine' tornado would carry on regardless.

The Dorset Cursus. Plan of the south-western section showing the relationships between the long barrows and the cursus. Some of the round barrows are indicated as well.
© *Crown copyright*

The path of the cursus then bears straight up the slope of Gussage Hill to the conspicuous long barrow (Gussage St Michael III) built crossways within the cursus on the hill crest.

After descending the far slope the cursus swerves slightly left, then right, and at the foot of the hill narrows before traversing a second broad valley, at which it bears left and crosses Wyke Down towards Bottlebush Down. At this point, on the slope where the cursus changes direction slightly, and now 5.6 kilometres from Thickthorn, a cross-bank with an outer ditch once existed, in a style that may have resembled a terminus, but it had been destroyed and its ditch filled in antiquity, possibly by the people who built it.

The cursus leaves the cross-bank with a slight change of direction and continues north-eastwards over the down. The original right-hand bank is visible here, following the field boundary and wire fence, as Richard Atkinson pointed out in 1955. Beyond the down the cursus crosses fields, swinging left and then right into a third valley, after which it enters a conifer plantation. Incorporated in the left-hand bank is a fairly well-preserved long barrow, called Pentridge IV. It is 43 metres long. Next the cursus runs fairly straight for a couple of kilometres, passing close to the village of Pentridge, and finishes on the level plain of Martin Down at a terminal earthwork which has been obliterated.

This northern structure had squared banks. Aligned on its centre are as many as three long barrows and a bank-barrow 152 metres long, suggesting that considerable importance was attached to this terminus, as to the southern end at Thickthorn. When the cursus is viewed as a whole, there is a surprising duplication of in-built alignments between the southern and northern parts, which would make sense if one imagined the work being carried out by co-operating tribal groups, one proceeding from the south and the other from the north, and that they met at Bottlebush!

Several writers have commented, without much enthusiasm, that cursuses may have been processional ways or funerary avenues, or that they may have served as enclosures or land divisions. A purely astronomical use was more energetically proposed by A. Penny and John Edwin Wood. Like previous workers, they assumed that the majority of long barrows were in place before the cursus was planned, and that it was cunningly woven between them, but the astronomical alignments are more likely to have been achieved by positioning the barrows after completing the cursus.

Analysis of snails found in the ditch bottoms suggests a combination of grassland and open beechwood, supported by the work of Richard Bradley who found that at points only 700 metres apart one length ran through mixed vegetation while another crossed a patch of closed woodland. A tornado would have created havoc with trees along its path and laid down a great number, but the clearance of broken, uprooted trees, besides scrub, would have still been a formidable task. Nonetheless, without the

The Dorset Cursus. Plan of the north-eastern section giving the relationships between the long barrows and the cursus. The positions of some round barrows are indicated, including Gussage All Saints 12 (GAS 12). © *Crown copyright*

aid of tornado destruction the labour would have been far greater. It is significant that the southern terminal is known to have been built in open grassland.

Is it likely that the cursus project was undertaken so that the powerful could exert their authority over the workers, as proposed by Richard Bradley? And with the aim of directing their attention to dummy mounds at the cursus terminals and nearby Wor Barrow, mounds which in earlier times had been intended as burial places but now were being built empty or nearly empty to demonstrate the might of the community leaders? While all these non-tornado suggestions are inadequate, some of them contain a degree of truth. The great cursus in Dorset is so preposterous in size, and so complex when examined, that outrageous explanations have been sought for it.

The tornado theory is simpler. The path of the Dorset Cursus, complicated though it is with its small changes of direction and width, agrees with all that is known of tornado trails as they rise over hills, cross streams and rivers, and tear through copses and forests. Like all British cursuses the Dorset Cursus would have been built without prior planning. Work would have begun immediately following a tornado strike. God had come down to earth.

As a result, cursus building was intrinsically straightforward—no surveying, no advanced planning, simply the hard grind of digging. Chance directed the tornado path and its trail through the woods, scrubland and fields, and mankind followed the course where it went. Except in times of war there never was greater motivation in the history of human endeavour than that promoted by religion, with its promise of life-after-death, as the supremely efficient way of exacting the maximum sweat and toil from mortals. Every cursus was made to be an everlasting memorial to a divine visit and at times may have been used for commemorative ceremonies and processions. Astronomical alignments and tribal prestige also came into this. Very full details concerning alignments and orientations within the Dorset Cursus complex may be found in *The Stonehenge Solution*.

The Tornado-Cursus God ploughed a vulva-like furrow in the soil, as the farmer did with his plough. Therefore, just as the Hindus, among others, identified the furrow with the vulva and the seeds with semen, so there existed a widespread identification among agrarian communities of woman or Goddess with the ploughed earth. Allusions to this belief survive to this day in European folklore. In the same way, the equation 'spade equals phallus' is so closely held that in some languages the roots of the words can only have been the same. There are many pictorial representations on the theme, like the Swedish rock-carving from Litsleby, which has the additional touch of a symbolic may-tree proffered by the man or god; the message of spring fertility extends even to the draught animals joined to the plough.

The Great Goddess was the fountain and source of life, and the Cursus God an occasional consort-impregnator, but when union between God and Goddess took place it was climactic—that atmospheric moment when Sky blended with Earth. For the

A Bronze Age rock carving from Litsleby in Western Sweden. The ithyphallic ploughman and 'oxen' are depicted cutting three furrows in the fields of Goddess Earth, each furrow a symbolic vulva. This (three furrow) agricultural rite was widespread in Europe and persisted well into Christian times in many regions.

affected locality it was an exultant day in the lore of the Goddess—a day demanding to be memorialised by the anxious community—because first and foremost the cursus was a Goddess monument, built in honour of the day when she visibly received the Cursus God in holy union. In recognising the event as an act of Divine Marriage the cursus was celebrating the founding of the universe and the creation of life itself.

How, then, does the cursus-tornado theory stand up to scrutiny? The majority of cursuses are shorter than two kilometres. Many are straight or composed of straight sections, sometimes with small deviations of direction or width. The 800 metres of the Thornborough cursus curve gently for the whole of its length. There is nothing in any of the cursuses which debars the possibility of their having been constructed by pursuing a tornado trail across the landscape. The small directional change that sometimes happens in the lee of a hill is familiar to tornado investigators, but as a property of the long Dorset Cursus this oddity has been a puzzle for cursus theorists.

Tornadoes which rip through a forest tear down the trees as they go. This very act, at once typical of the lofty whirlwind and Cursus God and which so terribly ravishes the Earth, immensely lightens the toil of forest clearance. The problem, sometimes voiced, concerning the need for the laborious removal of trees in the largely-forested

These Swedish rock carvings show the development of the idea, using images and symbols, that began with the cattle-drawn plough. Plough and spade being synonymous with penis, the wheeled farm implement is transformed into male genitalia, while the draught animals become the female opening. Simplicity reaches its logical limit in the picture below where the sexual organs are joined. So the action of ploughing proves to be equivalent to the consummation of marriage between Plough and Earth—as if between God and Goddess.

Early Neolithic landscape, believed to be essential before cursus building could begin, evaporates before the destructive whirlwind which cuts its corridor through the mixed vegetation and trees. Moreover, the tornado is oblivious of swamp and river. So, it would appear, is the cursus.

As we have seen, the Dorset Cursus traverses the marsh of Gussage St Michael and its chalk stream. The Stanwell/Heathrow cursus, 3.5 kilometres long and 20 metres wide, crosses two rivers, the Colne and the Wraysbury, west of Heathrow Airport. These rivers are deep and wide with a flood plain between, and there must have been a considerable amount of water in this part of the cursus four thousand years ago.

The Drayton cursus in Oxfordshire seems to be in two parts, formed by a tornado which lifted from the ground, crossed a stream and struck along the same line of attack a couple of hundred metres farther on. In Yorkshire one of the Rudston cursuses crosses a major chalk stream, the Gypsey Race.

In view of the importance attached to the religious meaning of cursuses—notably, their role in the mystical concept of the Marriage of the Gods—it would be natural for every community to want its own cursus as proof that it, too, had been favoured by a visitation from the Sky God, and that the Cosmic Union had taken place on its territory. I therefore started looking at parts of central southern Britain where cursuses seem to be lacking despite having been densely inhabited in Neolithic and Bronze Age times. The areas of chief interest were the Windmill Hill/Avebury region of North Wiltshire, and the region of South Dorset in the neighbourhood of Dorchester and Maiden Castle.

We know that the Dorchester area is extremely rich in all classes of monument from the Neolithic and Bronze Ages. Only a cursus is missing, and yet long barrows and bank barrows are present in much the same way as those which accompany the great cursus between Thickthorn and Pentridge in North Dorset. In *The Stonehenge Solution* a proposal is made, and fully documented, that a cursus one kilometre long once extended from the bank barrow on Long Bredy Down to the bank barrow of Kingston Russell.

From what is known of the archaeology of cursuses, and since their adoration spanned a thousand years of British prehistory, it would be surprising if the enormously influential Windmill Hill/Avebury region had not partaken in the religious practice of Cursus God idolatry which everywhere else in Britain was so intense. One need only look at the ancient monuments of the Thames Valley, which at one point passes not far north of the Windmill Hill area, to find that over half a dozen cursuses once existed in the valley between Lechlade and Middlesex. So why was there no ditch-and-bank cursus close to Windmill Hill?

It is worth considering whether the Neolithic megalithic avenue south of Windmill Hill, known as Beckhampton Avenue, was inaugurated for this purpose. In contrast to the Stonehenge area which was largely barren of good stone, huge sarsen blocks were liberally scattered across the Avebury region. Because a tradition of their use in chambered-barrow building had long existed, the Windmill Hill people may have translated the cursus concept of parallel banks-and-ditches into stone. The same could be postulated for some of the stone rows of Dartmoor, Exmoor, Wales and Western Scotland and the initial phases of stone-row construction at Carnac, Kerzerho, and elsewhere in France.

Only two stones of Beckhampton Avenue survive, but fortunately its course was recorded by William Stukeley in the eighteenth century. It is over two kilometres long and, according to Aubrey Burl and others, is the oldest part of the Avebury megalithic complex. Its sinuous progress accords with the facts of tornado theory, so the idea may be ventured that the stone avenue was built to follow a tornado path in order to mark it for eternity. This suggestion overcomes a problem which is otherwise difficult to explain. If the Windmill Hill people wanted to build a ceremonial way lined with megaliths out of free choice, why did they not choose easier ground and avoid the crossing of two watercourses? The engineering problems were already enormous without having to build wooden bridges and drag the gigantic blocks over them as well. One of the bridges had to be twenty metres long in order to cross the fifteen-metre wide stream, which meant the felling and transportation of huge trees. The problems are such as to suggest that the megalithic avenue builders had no choice regarding the route to follow—the Tornado-Sky God willed it on them.

The age of Beckhampton Avenue is unknown. The finding of a Beaker burial with a vessel of 24th century BC type, buried within a special three-stone setting called the cove, gives a latest possible date, because it means that the cove is at least this old, but it gives no clue as to how much older the cove might be than the beaker, nor how much older the avenue might be than the cove. All we can say is that, from what we know now, it is quite possible that the first of Avebury's processional megalithic avenues followed the winding trail marked out by a tornado in much the same way that the Calne tornado did on 30 December, 1859 and which also went close to Windmill Hill. Whereas the few surviving, mostly fallen, megaliths seen by William Stukeley were quite massive, it does not follow that all the avenue stones were huge. The missing stones could have been smaller than the familiar Avebury ones. After all, it would be the smaller stones which would be destroyed first, and the builders of an early, very long cursus-avenue comprising hundreds of stones might have preferred to use comparatively small megaliths to make their work easier, but including occasional exceptions like those at the entrance to the later henge and near the Beckhampton Cove. If so, the holes in the underlying chalk would be shallow and hard or impossible to detect by geophysical-survey techniques.

6

The Stonehenge Cursuses

Looking north from the stone circles of Stonehenge, one can see part of the 2.7-kilometre long monument that is the Stonehenge Cursus. This is the Greater Cursus, discovered by Dr William Stukeley on 6 August, 1723. But there is a Lesser Cursus as well, which is important both in itself and for several noteworthy, co-existing tornado parallels. Regrettably, the Lesser Cursus has vanished from sight.

Like so many cursuses subjected to centuries of plough action, the banks of the Lesser Cursus have been effaced. Nothing remains but transient cropmarks which appear over the former ditches during periods of dry weather. But the plough was not entirely responsible for erasing this cursus from the landscape; the main job was done in antiquity by Neolithic people who backfilled the ditches not long after digging them! When the remains of the Lesser Cursus were sighted by the alert Richard Colt Hoare, 180 years ago, enough was left of the banks for him to identify their positions. Since then the modern plough has removed even these slight traces.

The Lesser Cursus is 400 metres long and 50 metres broad. It lies 650 metres north-west of the western end of the Greater Cursus. Partial excavation in 1983 by Julian Richards proved that it was built in two stages. In the first the length was 200 metres, with shallow ditches 30 centimetres deep, ending in the east with a cross-bank.

In the second stage the ditches were deepened, and the cursus extended eastwards a further 200 metres, leaving an open end in place of a terminal ditch and bank. Then, soon afterwards, the cursus was closed down and the ditches filled with material from the banks—but leaving enough to survive until the nineteenth century AD, when Richard Colt Hoare spotted what remained.

While it will never be possible to know the full intentions of the builders, we can use the available evidence to suggest what may have happened. The initial size of the cursus and its orientation (from the west-south-west) conform with the straightness and uniform width typical of a short tornado track. Such tracks are easy to follow where they pass through a forest or a stand of trees. The middle cross-bank of the cursus could have marked the point of exit of the tornado from forest to grassland, after which the devastating wind disappeared across open fields.

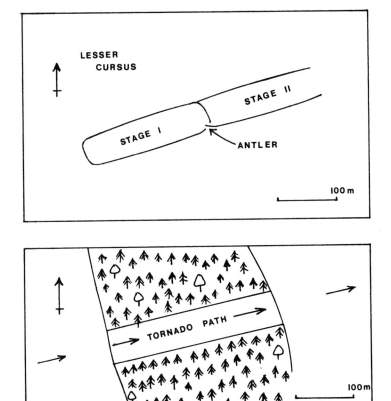

The Lesser Cursus at Stonehenge, and a comparison of its orientation and dimensions with those of the May 1979 tornado which tore a path through a tree plantation a few kilometres away on Ablington Down.

Aerial photograph of the tornado track which cut through the trees of the Ablington Down plantation near Stonehenge in May 1979. *Photo The Salisbury Journal*.

This suggestion is no idle speculation. Such an occurrence took place eight kilometres north-east of Stonehenge at 1320 GMT on 30 May, 1979. The tornado arrived from the west-south-west and destroyed 200 trees over a path fifty metres wide across the entire 300-metre length of the forty-year-old Wig Plantation on Ablington Down, above Figheldean. Because the ends of the track were rectangular where the tornado entered and left the trees, a square-ended enclosure or cursus would have resulted if landscape engineering had been attempted, based on the trail left by the Neolithic Sky God—for this is what appears to have happened in the Age of the Cursus when the cult of the Spiral-Tornado-Bull Cult was rising. For the first time in the locality of the Pre-Stonehenge People, the track left by the Tornado-Sky God was to be preserved as a major earthwork. The date was in the last quarter of the fourth millennium BC, a couple of centuries before the first earth was moved at Stonehenge.

The Lesser Cursus was originally built so far, but it seems that, after only a few months or years, the diminutive cursus was regarded as inadequate for the pride and needs of the community when compared with others in the south of Britain, particularly the Dorset Cursus. So the Lesser Cursus was deepened and elongated eastwards but left open-ended to indicate that the true length of the path taken by the Sky God was unclear. The tornado of 30 May, 1979, continues to provide the perfect parallel, because we know that it pursued an eastbound course over open country for a further kilometre before catching the tops of the next plantation as it was lifting and dissipating.

For some time the people probably had to be content with this small cursus, for want of anything better, but after some years the Sky God returned to mate again with the Goddess.

Striking the plain or forest 650 metres to the south-east, and in full view of eye-witnesses if it was daylight, another spiralling tornado sped eastwards. This more powerful whirlwind, on a slightly different orientation, left a damage track which led to the building of the Stonehenge Cursus. The devout farmers, inspired no doubt by the explanations of a priest or priestess, could now raise a monument truly worthy of the Tornado-Bull Cult—a grander monument which would compare more favourably with others of which they had heard tell.

The Stonehenge Cursus is a magnificent spectacle when viewed from either end or from the air. Its west-east orientation is typical of the direction taken by many British tornadoes. The length is 2.7 kilometres and its width, which varies, averages more than 100 metres, with the maximum of 130 metres half-a-kilometre from its western end. The ground undulates gently from the west as the cursus descends into a dry valley and rises again to the opposite terminal. Although the banks are much eroded, especially in the heavily ploughed eastern half, they are easy to follow on both sides of the western section.

It is believed that this cursus dates from at least the beginning of the henge of Stonehenge and probably earlier, in the last quarter of the fourth millennium BC. In fact, there is a high probability that it was founded at the same time that the Lesser Cursus was closed down. The discovery by J. F. S. Stone of a Grooved Ware sherd and of a 90-millimetre piece of Welsh Cosheston-Senni mica-bearing sandstone of Milford Haven type, from the base of the cursus ditch near Fargo plantation at the western terminal, indicates that the cursus was still in use well into the third millennium. Grooved Ware sherds, interred in a ritual pit, were found by William Hawley at the bottom of the ditch encircling Stonehenge, two adjoining sherds displaying chevrons. This pottery is characteristic of the middle part of the Neolithic era when the Goddess religion was in its ascendancy. Farther to the south-west, in Dorset, Richard Bradley has proved that the Stonehenge Cursus is younger than the immense Dorset Cursus, and the finding of third-millennium Beaker pottery there bears further witness to the long period of use enjoyed by cursuses in Southern Britain.

Exploratory excavations have been made at both terminal ends of the Stonehenge Cursus by Julian Richards and others. The bank outside the eastern end, at right angles to the cursus, which had always been regarded as an 81-metre long barrow (called

The chief Neolithic and Bronze Age monuments in the neighbourhood of Stonehenge and the cursuses. The nine long barrows which bear on the terminals of the Stonehenge Cursus are numbered in accordance with Table II. Round barrows are indicated by small closed circles; open circles mark the positions of destroyed barrows. © *Crown copyright*

Amesbury 42) was shown to have been raised by deepening the ditch of the true eastern terminal (since vanished) merely to imitate the mound of a long barrow. The bones of no less than four or five bulls (*Bos longifrons*), uncovered by John Thurnam in 1868, had already hinted at its true identity, 'and there may have been others not reached by the excavations. Altogether, the appearances justify the conclusion that oxen were slaughtered at the time of the obsequies for the funeral feast, and that the heads and feet, not being used for food, were thrown on the yet incomplete barrow, as offerings, to the *manes* or to other deities.'

But there were no interments, and no obsequies—because this was no burial barrow. It was part of the cursus, and the offerings could only have been dedicatory ones of the long-horned Neolithic bull. The bank was to honour the Sky God and to serve another purpose too (probably the reason why its height had been raised so effectively)—to provide a better sighting device to allow it to be seen over several kilometres. Much the same can be said for the unobstructed western terminal, whose height enabled it to be seen from afar. The proof lies in the extraordinary series of long-barrow alignments designed into the Stonehenge Cursus landscape.

There are sixteen long barrows within five kilometres of Stonehenge, and scholars have searched in vain for solar or lunar alignments in their orientations. Aubrey Burl states generally that long barrows were sited for the mound to be conspicuous. This is true of a large number of Wessex long barrows, including in the Stonehenge region the equinoctial barrow Figheldean 27 (Knighton Barrow) which is so well exposed on a hilltop three kilometres north-north-east of Stonehenge that it can be seen for many miles about.

All long barrows in the Stonehenge region were surveyed in order to gain the highest possible accuracy for their orientations, using a military compass accurate to half-a-degree. I was able to establish the orientations of the best preserved barrows with an accuracy of one degree, but for most others, reduced in height and broadened with age, plus or minus (±) two or three degrees was the limit.

With the single exception of the east-west barrow Figheldean 27 (Knighton Barrow), *all long barrows within sight of one or other end of the Stonehenge Cursus are aligned on one of the cursus terminals* (See Table II). *This is an amazing and far-reaching discovery*, which has been checked and confirmed by others in the last few years.

The rule applies unreservedly to seven of the long barrows in the table. The second and third barrows (Winterbourne Stoke 1 and Amesbury 14), which are close to the cursus and accurately aligned upon its western terminal, are just out of view due to small variations in the slope of the land, although the tops of neighbouring trees can today be seen. *It can only mean that the nine barrows were built after the event that prompted the building of the cursus, and signifies that the cursus was the focus of worship.* Figheldean 27, exposed on a hilltop in view of the cursus, is close to the ancient Robin Hood's Ball causewayed enclosure. *Because this one long barrow in sight of the cursus is not aligned on a terminal it probably predates the cursus.* The barrow Bulford 1, which is three kilometres east of the cursus, is excluded from the list because it cannot be seen from the cursus; nor can the equinoctial Wilsford 30 just south of Normanton Down.

A possible solar alignment links Figheldean 31 and Durrington 24 with the eastern end of the cursus. As seen from the northern end of the east-terminal bank the direction

TABLE II

Alignments between the Stonehenge Cursus and its long barrows

Barrow Name	Grid Ref	Length metres	Self-orientation	Bearing to terminal
THE LONG BARROWS ORIENTATED ON THE WESTERN TERMINAL				
1 Winterbourne Stoke 53	SU 09174280	32	E c87°	87°
2 Winterbourne Stoke 1	SU 10004151	74	NNE/NE 36°	34.5°
3 Amesbury 14	SU 11544176	31	SSE 154°	153°
THE LONG BARROWS ORIENTATED ON THE EASTERN TERMINAL				
4 Winterbourne Stoke 71	SU 10104090	c50	NE/ENE c58°	58°
5 Wilsford 34	SU 10414118	36	NE/ENE c56°	59°
6 Wilsford 13	SU 11894130	20	NE 44°	44°
7 Amesbury 140	SU 14184194	20	SSE c160°	162°
8 Durrington 24	SU 12474440	44	SE 135°	133°
9 Figheldean 31	SU 10894588	45	SE 135°	133°

NOTES

1   A tenth barrow, Amesbury 10a at SU 11944217 (west of Stonehenge), has been excluded because it is reported that ditches have not been detected on air photographs; however, the barrow is shown on earlier maps as elongated with a self-orientation of 60° which directs it at the eastern terminal's outer bank. So even if it is not a ditched long barrow, this 'long mound' may have been planned into the cursus barrow system.

2   Founder's Barrow. Winterbourne Stoke 1 held the skeleton of an old man (a chief?) with a shaped piece of flint 20 cm long (tornado replica?) at his right arm.

of these barrows is 312° to the nearest degree (but 313° when measured from its centre), whereas the prehistoric midsummer sunset azimuth was 311.5° for a view of the last tip of the setting sun's disc.

It is important to realise that the outer bank of the east terminal of the Stonehenge Cursus (formerly known as long barrow Amesbury 42) stands on land about two metres higher in elevation than where the cursus otherwise terminates. The people appear to have found that the cursus track finished inconveniently early and that the eastern terminus, as originally built, was obstructed from the east by the height of the nearby ridge. The objective was to place this additional 'sighting' monument on the brow of the ridge to increase its height and bring it within view of all six barrows which point at the eastern terminal.

From the west terminal the long barrow known as Winterbourne Stoke 53 is plainly visible end on. Its orientation is parallel to and aligned with the Stonehenge Cursus. Tornado theory suggests that the barrow was positioned to preserve the azimuthal direction from which the tornado funnel cloud arrived before it struck the ground or forest. This barrow was dug into by William Cunnington in the nineteenth century and found to contain evidence of unusually extensive burning prior to the raising of the mound. This could mean that bonfire beacons or funerary pyres heralded the construction of barrow and cursus, perhaps imitating the tornado funnel itself on anniversary dates.

The other long barrows which are accurately aligned on the western terminal (Winterbourne Stoke 1 and Amesbury 14), despite their closeness are just hidden by the brow of a low hill; their precise alignments could have been achieved with the aid of high posts or fires. The magnificent barrow Winterbourne Stoke 1, 74 metres long and adjacent to the busy A303 trunk road, is orientated on a bearing 36 ± 1–1.5°, and not on 41, the most northerly moonrise, as Aubrey Burl suggests in *The Stonehenge People*. In this barrow John Thurnam found what he took to be a phallus of flintstone. It lay close to the right arm of an old man buried at the eastern end with his head to the south-west. John Thurnam described the object as a 'bludgeon-shaped flint about eight inches long, and well adapted for being grasped in the hand. From one end numerous flakes had been knocked off, and it had evidently constituted an object of considerable importance to the owner'. Could this flint have been shaped to imitate the divine penis—the tornado funnel—of the Sky God, part of the paraphernalia of a religious ceremony connected with the monument? Was its owner the man who masterminded the prestigious cursus operation? Although this long barrow is orientated on the western terminal and not on any cosmically-possible moonrise, the round barrows which sprang up in a line north-east of the long barrow during the next thousand years had a common azimuth around 41°. This is the direction of extreme northerly moonrise as seen from the forecourt of the long barrow looking towards the knoll which constituted the local horizon.

Besides the copious evidence of bull sacrifice in the east-terminal bank of the cursus (the former Amesbury 42 long barrow), the Amesbury 14 long barrow which is aligned on the western terminal yielded the skull and feet of a bull. Apart from the barrows

The 20-centimetre flint found with a corpse in the Winterbourne Stoke long barrow (long barrow number 2 in Table II). The shape is both phallic and tornadic. Its position suggested to the excavator that it was a most treasured possession. Did it belong to the man who planned the building of the tornado-made cursus?

mentioned, no other cursus long barrows have been excavated, but numerous long barrows on the western half of Salisbury Plain (at least six, probably eight) have yielded *Bos longifrons* skulls, hooves and other bones, in addition to the skulls and feet from the mortuary long barrow known as Fussell's Lodge. Richard Colt Hoare, for instance, found seven or eight bull or ox-skulls in Boles Barrow (Heytesbury I). Farther north, towards Avebury, the excavation of a Bronze Age round barrow at Hemp Knoll by M. E. Robertson-Mackay uncovered a grave pit with the complete head and four hooves of a bull as an accompaniment to a Bell-Beaker burial. This proves that a form of Bull God worship persisted in Wessex for a very long time because a thousand years separate the building of these long and round barrows. The bovine remains from Hemp Knoll help to emphasise the ritual nature of the findings from the Salisbury Plain long barrows and the Stonehenge Cursus and, as we shall see, Stonehenge itself.

Contemporary with the bull-cult was the role of antler symbolism. The association of antlers with fertility aspirations originates in the perennial shedding and 'rebirth' of this hard-wearing material. Its appearance in the ditches of the two Stonehenge Cursuses, in Salisbury Plain earthen long barrows, in the Neolithic circular ditch of Stonehenge and in innumerable Early Bronze Age round barrows bears witness to something more than the carefree abandonment of a well-used tool upon the completion of chalk-ditch cutting. The logic of symbolism directs that the antler, some-

The head and four hooves of a bull which had been ritually buried in a Bronze Age round barrow at Hemp Knoll on the Beckhampton Downs in Wiltshire. A roe-deer antler was also found there.

times worn-out, sometimes virgin, was returned to Earth as a thank-offering to the divinity whose loan had eased men's labours, while simultaneously functioning as a fertility and rebirth symbol because of its rapid growth and uterine shape. On ceremonial occasions antlers would have served in fertility and funerary rituals, as they still do in surviving folk traditions from our ancient past, such as the annual Horn Dance at Abbots Bromley in Staffordshire, which is held in the first week of September.

* * *

Over five thousand years ago in Neolithic times, probably as far back as 3800–3000 BC, prodigious longitudinal monuments were being built across the face of Britain. Over hill and dale, sometimes crossing waterways, they meandered and wound, or went straight as a die. Cursuses are unique to Britain. No ditch-and-bank structures of enclosure type, built on such a scale, are known anywhere else in world prehistory; in Britain, however, principally in England, several dozen were built, with lengths mostly ranging from one to ten kilometres and breadths chiefly between 40 and 100 metres. But just as cursuses are rare in Scotland and Ireland, so do tornadoes occur very much less frequently than in England. The opportunity or insight for cursus-worship to develop in other countries therefore never arose, with one known exception: the anthropologist Fernando Ortiz has discussed at length the intense degree to which native Indians of Cuba and the southern and eastern parts of North America revered and worshipped the dangerous, spiralling tornado, waterspout and hurricane.

Since the discovery of the first cursus near Stonehenge in the eighteenth century, the cursus enigma has given archaeologists an exceptional and increasingly difficult challenge as the number of known examples has risen. Today, it is clear that, without external aid, archaeological resources will be insufficient to resolve the main problem: what sort of stimulus could drive men to desert their farms and pastures and labour for months on end with the idea of scouring deep ditches in chalk or limestone and piling up banks of such colossal length? Added to this are the problems of forest clearance and long-term maintenance.

Although documentary evidence will never be forthcoming, and all knowledge of myths and lore concerning the cursuses vanished thousands of years ago, it is probable that the major force behind cursus building was religion. It has been thought that British Neolithic religion was a realm so dark and remote as to be beyond the reach of any anthropologist or religious historian; nevertheless, this book shows that an interpretation combining religion with meteorology can account for all the major features of the cursuses and can provide a good base for myth-building, too. Such large-scale earthwork construction could scarcely be achieved without the advice and authority of a priest-led or at least priest-assisted powerbase. No shamanic individual or religious community leader or godless chieftain could command the influence that would mobilise the workforce for years or decades at a time. But families of devout, pious farmers would respect the opinions of priests and priestesses who could offer celestial explanations in conformity with prevalent belief, explanations which would not challenge but would sustain the needs of a simple agrarian society.

A universal motif commonplace in primitive mythologies portrays the divine couple Sky and Earth, or Sun and Moon. Appearing at the focus of creation myths, they supply the spiritual understanding of a cosmic scene in which Earth is revered as the mother deity and Sky is the father deity. Their marriage enriches the world and gives birth to all life-forms. The powers of the sky gods originate from their fertilising capacities which they owe to their gift of life-bringing rain. Goddess Earth responds by succouring the seeds and causing them to emerge as grass and cereals. Every rainstorm is a cosmic event welcomed for its life-bearing gifts, but in the thunderstorm is the godhead about which lightning darts and thunderbolts and hailstones scream to the ground. Here is the Sky God in his manifestation of Storm God where he boasts his strength and bellows like a bull. And when he lowers his twisting funnel to the ground—his anticlockwise spiral of destruction—that is when his potency and masculinity are savagely and terrifyingly apparent.

In conspicuous union with Earth he scars the forest and field, and only the Earth Goddess survives the onslaught. All else yields to the spiralling wind, and a track of devastation remains for mortals to meditate on. Every community understood the spiritual message; and because each came to desire and expect such a 'visitation from the sky' the religious leaders ensured that the Cosmic Consummation, when it came, would be commemorated by a Cyclopean earth-moving project.

Archaeology dates the chief era of the building and exploitation of cursuses from the second quarter of the fourth millennium to the end of the third millennium—around 1,500 years. An association with Grooved Ware has been found at some cursuses, early henges and stone circles. Aubrey Burl comments that, because Grooved Ware appeared in the context of a new ritual, the ceramic deposits were symbols of a new cult; but he concluded 'we shall never know the ethos of this cult'. The Bull-Sky God cult in connection with the tornado revelation may partly answer this question. More will be inferred by re-analysing the significance of excavated objects and bones in the context of ritual and domestic activity, and much has been learnt from studying cursus dimensions, shapes, directional changes and orientations, and the siting and contents of related, neighbouring monuments. Using a socio-religious approach which includes the role of atmospheric powers in the choreography, a small part of the religious fabric of these ancient times has been clarified.

The cursus was the creation of the Sky God, a roaring bull with spiralling spout, thunderbolts and hailstones, his worship ritualised through offerings of bull's heads, horns, antlers, phalluses, discs and balls. We can admire a British cursus in its symbolic context and ponder over its spiritual implications. It is the ancient Briton's supreme tribute to the gods, an everlasting memorial to the day they met on earth—an occasion celebrated annually forever after, at the place where the consummation took place. A cursus was a priestly monument, the biggest construction in the Neolithic world dedicated to Sacred Marriage. Ritual rings of pits and posts, henges and megalithic rings followed afterwards, but all the while the cursuses proclaimed to newcomers the ancient rights to land-use and tenure held by the lineal descendants of the cursus-builders—those ancestors who had witnessed the coming of the Sky God in the remotest past.

William Stukeley's choice of the word *cursus* has proved to be a shrewd and happy one because the ditch-and-banked cursus was, as he guessed, a course or way which must at times have attracted events that assumed a processional character. But the cursus was no secular avenue; it was consecrated to the most potent divinities of the spiritual world in commemoration of their sacred meeting. The point of entry, the 'landing terminal', was the Gate of the Gods, and the point of departure was a second Gate. Therefore the cursus was the divine way, the Path of the Gods. That same path leads to understanding the secrets of the meaning of the stones of Stonehenge, and the answers to the question: why was Stonehenge built?

7

The Henge of Stonehenge is Born

About the year 1666 John Aubrey wrote in the manuscript of his book *Monumenta Britannica*: 'I am now come to Stone-heng, one of our English Wonders, that hath been the subject of so much Discourse'. More than three hundred years later, and through the centuries between, the discourse has not ceased. Despite considerable advances on the archaeological front the main problems have not been cracked. Why was the monument built? What did it represent? How did it function?

The reason why Stonehenge has not yielded its ultimate secrets is because no one has succeeded in reading the minds of those who built it. To decipher the monument, we must restore elements of the lost religion and rediscover the essential myth of the times. Scholarship in the study of early religions proves that the prevalent belief centred on a female deity, the Great Goddess, and that a crucial component of the mythology was the rite of Sacred Marriage. Not only did this concept glorify the Goddess to an exceptional degree, but it embraced, to a lesser extent, her marriage partner the Sky God as well.

The great cursus at Stonehenge was still in use when work began on the first Stonehenge. The digging of the circular ditch came first: the purpose was to raise a bank to enclose the sacred area. The irregular ditch consisted of short sections which, to judge by their lack of symmetry, seem to have been dug simultaneously by separate gangs and the sections joined by breaking down the intervening walls. We know this from the excavations of William Hawley who spent several seasons at the monument in the 1920s.

The beginnings of Stonehenge date from the start of the third millennium BC. Radio-carbon testing on stag-horns from the base of the great circular ditch dates them to around 3000 BC. This corresponds with the digging of the ditch according to both William Hawley and Richard Atkinson because the ditch was never subsequently back-filled; it silted up slowly and naturally over succeeding centuries.

Two causeways were left when digging the ditch: a major one at the north-east in the general direction of midsummer sunrise and a lesser one at the south. The north-east entrance is the ceremonial and holy entrance to the sacred space of the circles. The southern entrance was possibly intended as a secular point of entry, like the back door of a church.

Most of the chalk rubble cast out from the ditch was used to raise a circular bank on its inside, of diameter 93 metres. A causewayed circular monument of this type, of which there are more than seventy in Britain, is known today as a henge (Stonehenge being the site which gave rise to the name). The most prominent feature at this time was a massive megalith, the Heel Stone, placed outside the bank on the north-east side where it still stands, probably in its original position, for Richard Atkinson and Aubrey Burl are agreed that the Heel Stone was set up at the very birth of the first Stonehenge. A pottery sherd of Windmill Hill type, which is early Neolithic, was found near the bottom of its stone-hole, showing that the Heel Stone corresponded to the oldest period of the monument. The top of this solitary stone is somewhat rounded but it seems that no attempt was ever made to modify its shape, its coarse ruggedness bearing witness only to the repeated onslaught of frost and weather.

Considerable speculation has surrounded the reasons for the choice of the site at Stonehenge, much of it astronomical. It is important to know what constructions were there in the earliest stages. Luckily archaeology has provided us with useful if incomplete clues. If we can decide what was planned into the design at the beginning, we can more aptly pose the question, why?

We can at least be clear on what was there during the early period, until the time when the first stone circles were being raised around 2550 BC. Besides the big bank, ditch and Heel Stone there were probably four megaliths: the two 'station stones' surrounded by their own smaller circular banks and ditches, and two other 'station stones' without ditches. There is also excellent evidence for a central structure of wood at this early stage. The 56 Aubrey Holes, located a short distance inside the peripheral circular bank and set on a ring 85 metres in diameter, belong to this period as well.

What was at the centre of the great grass-covered circle in its early days? In his book *The Stonehenge People*, Aubrey Burl presents a good case for a circular building made of timber with an inner wall of diameter thirty metres and an outer wall slightly greater than this—about 31 metres. These diameters are only slightly smaller than the diameter of the sarsen stone circle which was raised about five hundred years afterwards. Several of the holes for the posts which supported the wooden structure have been excavated. One of them had been cut into when a stone-hole was being prepared for Stone 12 of the later sarsen ring, around 2500 BC.

An avenue of posts leading to the wooden edifice from the southern causeway suggests a rear entrance to a twin-walled construction. The size of the main posts of the building can be judged from one of the post-holes into the chalk rock, which was 1.2 metres deep and 0.8 metre across. It had been packed hard with rammed chalk. The result of William Hawley's work led Aubrey Burl to conclude that the building was once thatched and that it had an opening to the north-east and a lesser entrance to the south. The latter was approached by a non-straight wooden passage which may have been roofed. Why was it thought necessary to have the wooden construction facing north-east?

Since the site of Stonehenge is on sloping ground, a more fundamental question is this: why was such an awkward site chosen for consecration? Could it have been the deliberate choice of a priestess or priest for some arbitrary reason that will never be fathomable, or was it a decision dictated by the intervention of some extraordinary circumstance—much as the tornado path ordained the location of the cursus, a site hallowed of itself because it was decided by Nature, otherwise recognised as the Goddess?

Such an occasion, deemed portentous, might have been the sighting of a spiralling whirlwind. Throughout history whirlwinds have been regarded with alarm and mysticism, or at best with curiosity. Some peoples thought a whirlwind to be an exhalation from the earth, that is, from the Goddess's womb, and a worthy place at which to carry out anniversary and other rites. Whatever the reasons for site selection may have been, the monument took the form of a circular bank of earth and chalk rubble laid out as a 93-metre ring. The bank marked the area of sanctity, the ditch serving as a quarry for the contents of the bank. Moreover, right from the beginning, a link was established between this infant henge and the midsummer sunrise and the most northerly moonrise, because a causeway was left in the ditch and bank. And when the central wooden building went up, it faced midsummer sunrise whose general direction was indicated by placing a sarsen stone with rounded top outside the bank. It would help if we knew what it was called—perhaps it was the equivalent of Sun Stone or Shadow Stone, Phallus Stone or Stone of Life—but for the last three hundred years it has been known as the *Heel Stone*.

The essential elements of the scenario for the period 3000 to 2550 BC are complete. The sun rises on midsummer morning at its most northerly point along the eastern

Elements present, but not necessarily simultaneously, in the first phase of Stonehenge, and appropriate for the period 3000–2550 BC. There was a wooden structure at the centre, perhaps a simple ring of posts at first or the elements of a more substantial building. The Heel Stone lay at the extreme edge of the chalk causeway which was aligned on neither the midsummer-sunrise axis nor a major lunar axis, but was broad enough to allow observance of both solar and lunar risings at the most northerly parts of their cycles. There was also the ring of Aubrey Holes which followed the perimeter just inside the ditch and may or may not have held posts at some stage.

horizon, shines upon the open north-eastern side of the timber shrine and illuminates its interior. The waiting faithful would know that all was well with the world, that the season was on time, that midsummer's day had arrived. The full significance of this spectacle is considerable and is explained in the next chapter, but there are major questions to discuss first.

Although the Heel Stone nearly corresponds with the point of midsummer sunrise five thousand years ago, in a direction which is rather less than 50 degrees east of north, it is positioned on the right-hand side of the causewayed approach as seen from the centre of Stonehenge. The main breadth of the causeway is well to the north of what one might expect, the axis directed at 46° 33′ from north. Why should this be? One possibility was to allow the approach of a procession from a direction which would not interfere with celestial happenings along the sacred midsummer axis. But it is also possible that the causeway was skewed in order to permit the light of the moon, when rising at its extreme northerly point of its 18-year cycle, to radiate along the causeway towards the central monument. Aubrey Burl discusses this fully in *The Stonehenge People*. However, the skew is not exact, probably because the moon was not rising at its most northerly point in the year when the chalk was being split and lifted from the ditch.

The suggestion that the siting of the first Stonehenge arose by chance explains the long-standing puzzle regarding its rather poor location. The ground is neither flat nor high. A place a couple of hundred metres away would have greatly improved the general aspect towards the horizon. From Stonehenge the ground slopes into a shallow, dry valley which is often mist-filled around dawn in quiet, fine weather, even in midsummer. The slope was sharp enough to pose construction problems for the wooden building which, on the basis of the post-hole sizes and their arrangement, some archaeologists believe was roofed. Aubrey Burl's suggestion, that the site had the advantage of being approximately midway with respect to the cursus and that the whole of the cursus could be seen from it, is an excellent one, although, as he says, if these were the only objectives, a small shift of the site would have improved its location still more. A few hundred metres to the north the land is level, higher, and the cursus can still be seen. Dr Burl's opinion is that a location midway along the cursus was the deciding factor, although if this is so its misalignment of 75 metres from the cursus centre amounts to an error of 75 metres in the cursus half-length (one half of 2774 metres), which is four per cent. If exactness had been important, the mistake was needless because the Neolithic people could survey much better than this when they wished. More relevant is the fact that the midsummer orientation from Stonehenge is not directed towards any obvious part of the cursus. Despite cursus and henge being contemporary, and although they both glorify the sexuality of the Goddess, the site of Stonehenge was not chosen to orientate the Heel Stone on either terminal of the cursus.

The principal feature of Stonehenge at this time was the midsummer alignment of the Heel Stone with the henge centre. Every June the sun returned, and the orientation re-created its effect. The midsummer celebration was an annual affair bringing joy to the hard-pressed peoples of those times. I do not take the view that Stonehenge was a gloomy place, built with a central mortuary house and intended mainly for funeral processions. However, there may well have been a charnel house of some sort at the henge centre at some period, or even at the outset. But if the dead were left to rot in the central building as Aubrey Burl suggests, then it is more likely that they were there for the purpose of being reborn. Dr Burl stresses the importance of the moon and its motions, and in this context one should note that near the Heel Stone there are post-holes suggesting that at some stage the directions of the rising moon were being monitored. Astronomically the argument is valid, but we must remember that the moon moves in an 18.6-year cycle with regard to its rising and setting directions. Only in every nineteenth year would the moon rise at its most northerly point and in the Age of Stonehenge lives were short; few people survived beyond the age of thirty to forty. For much of their short lives the Stonehenge people had no extreme northerly moonrise to witness, but the sun kept returning, shining past the Heel Stone at every midsummer festival. So it is more probable that the purpose of the henge, even in its earliest days, was to exploit the activity of the sun which contributed to a festive ritual every June, an event of cosmic importance which brought security and happiness to a hard-working community.

8

The Marvel of the
Stonehenge Alignment

For about 450 years Stonehenge maintained its stoneless centre. The few stones at the site occupied peripheral positions near bank and ditch. Only from about 2550 BC, near the end of the Neolithic, were there stones in the central area, and it was only about 2500 BC that the great sarsens arrived.

These are the stones first noticed by visitors as they approach the monument on Salisbury Plain. At first appearing small in the distance, they vanish from view as the visitor drops beneath the low hill. Then, as the stones come into sight again, they loom from the landscape grandly and impressively, and this time the solitary Heel Stone beyond the main group to the north-east is easily seen, too. Among these great stones are the small bluestones from Wales, which remain scarcely visible until the visitor is almost on top of the monument.

The stones of Stonehenge have been much disturbed. Some are broken, many are missing, and most others are pitted or damaged by the passage of time. There was a melancholy period when visitors to Stonehenge took hammers with them, or hired them from Amesbury, that they might remove a piece of stone for themselves; and it is likely that bits of broken stone from the monument lie sadly in walls or gardens or beneath the metalled road which runs so hideously close by it.

Stonehenge as it is now, with many central stones damaged, fallen or missing. Shaded are the Heel Stone, the Altar Stone and the four peripheral 'station stones'. The filled-in part of the surrounding ditch at the entrance causeway is also shaded.

It is worth looking at a plan of the stones as they lie now, together with the original banks and the start of the midsummer-sunrise avenue, in comparison with a reconstruction which shows the arrangement at the end of the final stone-moving phase, not later than 1900 BC.

The stones lie in the centre of the area enclosed by the circular bank and external ditch, still with its original diameter of 93 metres. Measured across its outer edge, the diameter of the stone circle is nearly 32 metres. The north-east causeway links the

Stonehenge with the central stones in their final arrangement, about 1900 BC, but with the visible earthworks (the banks and ditches) shown largely as they are now. The positions of the 56 Aubrey Holes are indicated but not the Y and Z holes.

stones of the central area with the straight earth-banked avenue. A thousand years earlier the axis of the causeway had been 46° 33′, but when the avenue was built and made to align with the midsummer sunrise the axis was modified to agree with both, namely 49° 54′ 40″.

The innermost sanctum is formed into the shape of an open-ended ellipse, or U-shape, by the arrangement of five trilithon arches axially aligned on the midsummer sunrise. They are sarsen, a sandstone harder than granite, brought at least thirty kilometres from the region between Avebury and Marlborough in the north of Wiltshire. These stones are graded in height so that the biggest pair of upright stones, one weighing fifty tonnes and towering almost seven metres above ground level, forms the apex of the U-shape which is completed by two opposing pairs of stones of lesser but equal height, the shortest being at the tips of the U. Including the thickness of the lintel, the height of the great trilithon is 7.4 metres, which compares with 6.2 metres for the shortest of the trilithons.

This arrangement provides an imposing backdrop for what is the focus of the entire edifice—the Altar Stone. This stone, which used to be the most splendid of all the megaliths, was misnamed in the seventeenth century by the fancy of Inigo Jones, Surveyor Royal to King James I. The Altar Stone lies sadly prone, broken and largely hidden by the fall of the lintel and one upright of the great trilithon. To make matters worse, the great weight of the stones lying on it has pushed it deeply into the ground so that only its upper surface can be seen today. But at one time this stone rose proudly three metres high, and stood perpendicular to the solar axis four metres in front of the great trilithon that was later to destroy it. The Altar Stone is one of Stonehenge's foreign stones, made of a fine-grained, pale green mica-bearing sandstone from the Cosheston Beds that jut into the coast of Milford Haven in south-west Wales, nearly 300 kilometres distant. When scraped, microscopic mica mirrors are exposed which make the rock glint in the sunshine. *This raises the first of two major questions which have to be resolved* by anyone seeking to explain the iconography of Stonehenge: Why should this particular type of stone, from so far away, have been selected for the focal position of the Neolithic masterwork?

Including the Welsh Altar Stone, there were formerly perhaps as many as eighty stones at Stonehenge which were alien to the county of Wiltshire. These were the bluestones, all unquestionably of Welsh origin and whose hue 'mystically' deepens when wetted. In their final settings they occupied two groups—one a carefully composed U-shape of nineteen stones within the great trilithon group, the other a rather hastily-erected circle of sixty bluestones between the great trilithons and the outer ring of lintelled sarsens. But long before this reconstruction took place, towards 1900 BC, the bluestones had stood elsewhere in Stonehenge's sanctuary, and it was for that purpose that they had originally been brought there around 2550 BC.

The outer ring of sarsen stones, those first seen by today's visitors as they approach the monument, consists of thirty upright 26-tonne stones with thirty lintels forming a perfect circle. Although the site on which Stonehenge was built slopes towards the east, nevertheless the heights of the outer-ring uprights were so arranged that the lintelled circumference was almost precisely level. The diameter of this outer ring of stones is about one third of the overall diameter of the site.

Beyond the circular bank and ditch remains that primitive and basic feature of the monument, the rugged, isolated Heel Stone. An explanation for its shape and position

The trilithon with dagger carvings towards the base of the left-hand stone, illuminated by the summer evening sunshine.

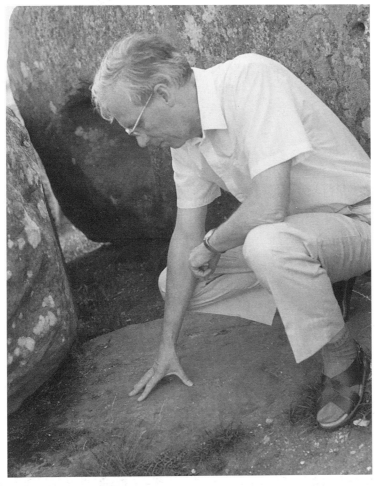

The 'Altar Stone' or, more exactly, Goddess Stone, lies recumbent and buried—pressed into the ground by the weight of the stones of the great trilithon which felled it.

is crucial if the riddle of Stonehenge is to be solved. During thousands of years of weathering it has acquired a cracked, uneven surface, but its general outline is much the same as when it was first put into use in the third millennium BC. Nonetheless, one far-reaching change has taken place, and that has been a progressive tilting away from the vertical, for the stone now leans markedly towards the monument.

If, as Richard Atkinson and Aubrey Burl believe, the Heel Stone has not been dressed, we may safely assume that it was carefully selected for its size and shape. Its present height is close to 4.7 metres, but restored to the vertical the apex would

Side view of the Heel Stone, showing the extent to which it is leaning from the vertical.

rise an additional 0.5 metre. From a ground-level width of 2.4 metres, as seen from the south-west, the stone tapers until near the top it becomes quite rounded. Viewed from the centre of Stonehenge the shape is so obviously phallic that, despite a lack of evidence of phallic worship at this place, this aspect has been commented upon from time to time.

Perhaps because so much has been written about the importance of sunrise alignments at Stonehenge, most people are surprised to learn that the Heel Stone does *not* point to the rising of the midsummer sun, not could it ever have done so in any past age. As an astronomical indicator the Heel Stone direction is no better than an approximate marker.

Today, if one watches the midsummer sunrise from a position standing on the main axis in front of the Altar Stone and looking directly up the avenue—that is, straight through the centre of the middle trilithon arch—the Heel Stone is not centrally framed within the arch as most photographers of the midsummer sunrise would have it appear. Furthermore, the tip of the sun shows to the left of the stone, and then passes to the right as the full orb comes into view. Because the Heel Stone protrudes so little above the tree-covered horizon, the sun is not much obstructed by the stone as it goes past (at most by ten per cent). It is at this moment that most photographers take their pictures.

There are several reasons why this view of the midsummer sunrise differs from what used to be seen in the Age of Stonehenge, the most obvious being caused by

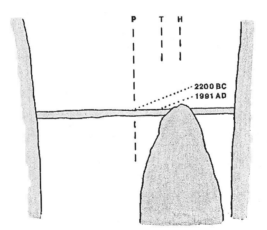

The leaning Heel Stone as seen from the Altar Stone today by an observer whose eye level is about 1.55 metres above present ground level. P marks the direction of the prehistoric sunrise for about 2200 BC, T gives the direction of sunrise today, and H is the Heel Stone direction. The course followed by the upper limb of the sun is indicated for 2200 BC and the present day.

the present-day slant of the Heel Stone. To correct for this, in makeshift fashion, the modern observer and photographer may try crouching or sitting instead, because this has the effect of raising the apparent elevation of the apex of the Heel Stone as seen from the centre of the monument. This explains why, since 1986, I have taken to lying or sitting with my camera at the centre of Stonehenge facing the midsummer sunrise. From this position, whereas the solar apex still comes into sight just to the left of the Heel Stone, the sun now goes wholly out of sight behind the stone rather than passing close to its top. A proper allowance for the inclination of the Heel Stone from the vertical is obviously needed, but the choreography is also confused by the important fact that in prehistoric times the midsummer sun did not rise where it does today.

At the midsummer solstice the sun now rises in a direction of nearly half a degree to the north of the Heel Stone's azimuth (50° 54′), but in the Age of Stonehenge it rose even farther to the north than that. The azimuthal drift of the point of the midsummer sunrise eastwards along the horizon results from an astronomical effect called the precession of the equinoxes. Since the year 2000 BC this has affected the position of sunrise by rather more than a solar diameter, the rate of movement along the horizon amounting to about 0.2 of a degree every thousand years.

On the other hand, within the limits of measurable accuracy we know that the axis of Stonehenge is aligned with the axis of the Stonehenge Avenue (49° 54′ 40″), which itself corresponds to the prehistoric solstitial sunrise for the end of the third millennium BC, if one supposes that the horizon was tree-covered as it is now. The Heel

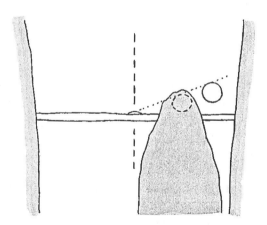

Revised sketch demonstrating the effect of straightening up the Heel Stone. This is approximately how the Heel Stone would have appeared to a prehistoric observer from a position in front of the Altar Stone. Shortly after sunrise at the midsummer solstice the sun would be eclipsed as it passed behind the Heel Stone.

Stone's position is to one side of this common axis. Therefore an observer at the centre of Stonehenge, at the time when the monument was designed and built, must have seen the sun rising freely over the tree-lined horizon, unaligned with and unobstructed by the Heel Stone.

The second fundamental question to be answered, then, is why did the designers and worshippers not bother to fix the Heel Stone precisely on the Stonehenge/Avenue/ sunrise axis if it was the axis that was so supremely important? Can it be true, as some investigators have suggested, that the later builders were content with the relatively crude positioning which their ancestors had seemingly accepted?

Aubrey Burl has tried to answer this by suggesting that around 3000 BC, at the founding of the earliest Stonehenge, when the peripheral banks and ditches were made and the axial direction of the north-east causeway was set at 46° 33', it was sufficient that the bearing of the Heel Stone should only approximate to midsummer sunrise, although the Heel Stone was over one degree east of the 3000 BC sunrise and the causeway axis was as much as three degrees north. This, he claims, was because it was the moon, not the sun, that was of primary interest. Following John Edwin Wood, he pursues the idea that the Heel Stone had been located about midway between maximum northerly moonrise (40–41°) and minimum northerly moonrise (60–61°) in order to signal about four or five years in advance when measurements of the direction of the extreme northerly moonrise should commence (the two extremes being separated by an interval equal to half 18.6 years). In those early days, before the orientation of the causeway was modified, the Heel Stone stood on the right side of the causeway and the most northerly moonrise lay in the direction of the left side. So it could be thought that the builders intended by their action to get both lunar and solar events into the scenario.

Yet the basic problem has been dodged, not answered. Why should the planners be so careless about fixing the solar direction when it was extremely easy to be exact about it? More pertinently, why was the misalignment of the Heel Stone with the solstice, if that is what it was, not corrected, either when the Welsh bluestones came to Stonehenge, about 2550 BC, or at a later date when the mighty sarsens were delivered? If more than a million and a half man-hours could go into rebuilding the monument, why was not a single day spent heaving the Heel Stone a couple of metres north-westwards? This point is crucial and *must be explained* by anyone seeking to explain the riddle of Stonehenge.

No answer has ever been forthcoming, and yet it is really very simple. The Heel Stone was not moved *because it was already in the right place*! From the moment it was set in its present stone-hole it has been achieving exactly what it was intended to do. And the secret vanished with the death of the last of the worshippers at Stonehenge more than three thousand years ago. The reason why the Heel Stone had to be located east of the midsummer sunrise position answers a very basic question relating to the primary motives behind the erection of the monument that is Stonehenge.

The non-alignment of the Heel Stone with the midsummer sunrise is instantly explicable if it is supposed that the intention was to view the actual rising of the sun followed by its immediate eclipse by the same stone. The builders either worked this out exactly before settling on the position of the Heel Stone or they arrived at the intended arrangement after trial and error, during which the stone temporarily occupied holes other than its present one. It can certainly be no accident that the Heel Stone is exactly the right size and is at just the right distance beyond the circular earthwork to throw its round-topped shadow to the heart of the monument.

It is unfortunate for the modern observer that after so many centuries the Heel Stone is leaning badly from the vertical. It is essential to determine the apparent elevation of the vertical Heel Stone just as it was in prehistoric times when the stone circles were prepared. At the time of the first bluestone rings it would have been 5.2 metres tall. Clearly, the height to which the sun becomes concealed by the stone is appreciable but it is not so much the view of the sun relative to the Heel Stone which is important; the crucial point is to what extent the Altar Stone gets subjected to shade. Therefore, inverting the procedure and looking at the situation from the opposite direction—that is, by considering what happens at the Altar Stone itself, we find by comparing relative

Awaiting the Midsummer Marriage. The Heel Stone projects above the horizon, as it was intended to do when positioned by the Stonehenge People. A jackdaw perches on top as the moment of sunrise approaches.

heights of Heel Stone and Altar Stone that a shadow at least 1.25 metres high cast by a vertical Heel Stone falls upon the three-metre high Altar Stone.

We also need to consider any effects that might result from the chemical solution of the sub-soil chalk rock by the flow of percolating rainwater during the course of four thousand years. Richard Atkinson estimates a lowering of 0.54 metres (although I have reason to believe that this is too much), combined with a surface level change of five millimetres caused by recent soil and turf level movements. Nevertheless, whatever the solution rate may reasonably be, it is doubtful whether it could lead to any significant difference in the amount by which the Altar Stone gets shadow-covered, for there will be no significant relative change of height between Heel Stone and Altar Stone anyway. The three-metre high stone will still have its lower part in shadow while the upper part remains in the sunshine. We can therefore reconstruct the prehistoric arrangement of sun and Heel Stone at sunrise on midsummer's morning, as it was intended by the bluestone-ring builders and the sarsen-ring builders between 2550 BC and 1600 BC. Their aim was to have the sun wholly eclipsed by the Heel Stone shortly after an unimpeded sunrise. It was an 'eclipse trick'.

It is the key to the solution of Stonehenge.

We may be sure that since the Heel Stone was set in place its shadow has reached to the centre of the monument on midsummer morning, and that since the Altar Stone arrived, the lower half of this vertical stone has been shadow-covered as well. Despite the thousands of drawings and models in reconstructions of Stonehenge that have been made, which show the stone lying horizontally, it was never intended to lie flat as true Altar Stones do. It was positioned vertically so that the shade of the Heel Stone should fall upon it.

Because the Heel Stone has probably been in its present stone-hole since the founding of the original henge, it looks as though the eclipse trick was designed into the primordial phase of Stonehenge when, as Aubrey Burl has so persuasively argued, a stoneless centre was occupied by a timber construction, open to the north-east but with a back-door entrance from the south, the two entrances being in line respectively with the north-eastern and southern causeways. Whether the building was a charnel house or Goddess shrine (perhaps with a north-east entrance similar to those of chambered barrows), the same argument holds. The skulls of bulls 'or other beasts' found in the central area in 1620 are the offerings of a society with beliefs in a bull-cult. That the people of the age were engaged in the cult of this animal is quite clear because of the great number of long barrows which conceal dedicatory offerings of the heads of bulls or the antlers of stags, besides which there is the unequivocal evidence of the cursuses. As we have seen, the cult of the bull is manifestly interwoven with the worship of both Great Goddess and Sky God, the horned bull providing the communicating link between heaven and earth and aiding the dead on their journey to the Other World. The bull's head and the stag's horns are not dismal signs of the dead but staunch images of hope and rebirth due to their well-recognised uterine symbolism within the context of a Goddess-centred religion.

So whatever structure was at the centre of Stonehenge at its earliest phase, whether shrine or charnel house for the dead, it must have been a focus for prayer and devotion, as well as for the light of the midsummer rising sun—except that it had been arranged that this light was soon extinguished by the eclipsing Heel Stone. This post-sunrise eclipsing alignment was retained when the bluestones came to Stonehenge a few hundred years afterwards. In fact, the people were so satisfied with the old position of the Heel Stone that they dug a circular ring around it to emphasise its sanctity and to distance the profane. With the bluestones came the gigantic Welsh Altar Stone with its glittering mica platelets, and this megalith was given the place of honour in the middle of Stonehenge, on the axis of the monument a little to the south-east of centre at what would have been viewed as the Centre of the World. From this moment onwards the Altar Stone became the most important of all the internal stones, even after the later arrival of the 75 great sarsens when Stonehenge was rebuilt after 2500 BC. The bluestone circles begun about 2550 BC were in fact never finished. They came down because a more grandiose scheme was started. The enormous trilithons went up, the position of the Altar Stone was shifted only slightly along the axis, and the outer ring of sarsens followed, joined to each other by touching lintels. All the time, the Heel Stone stayed where it was—locked in the perfect eclipsing position.

The reason for the special selection of the Altar Stone—which is in effect a Goddess Stone—and for bringing it so far from Wales, is due to its singular quality that when it is freshly scraped and washed its myriads of tiny mirrors shine red in the light of the rising sun—until the reflected rays are visibly extinguished by the advancing shadow of the Heel Stone. Because of the weakness of the solar rays at sunrise this optical trick allowed the arrival of the shadow to be more readily watched. This answers the basic question raised earlier as to why such an exceptional piece of rock should be brought so far for this unique location.

At sunrise the sun at first illuminates the entire stone and the cosmic mating commences. Then the shadow arrives and spreads across its bottom half, leaving the upper part in the sunlight.

While a large number of spectators, their backs to the sun, could have been viewing this miracle of optics from within the holy of holies, only very few other privileged attendants could have been in a position to watch the sun vanishing behind the vertical Heel Stone. They would have seen the sun's full diameter disappear, only to reappear after an interval of two or three minutes or so (depending on the height of the observer). But this was not so important as watching the Altar Stone glinting in the rising sun, and then seeing its lower half darken as the phallic shade encroached, before glowing again in the sunlight. The supreme climax had come and gone.

By about 1900 BC the smaller bluestones, whose positions had been changed on

12. Viewed from near
the top of the Heel Stone,
the shadow is seen reaching
the right-hand side of the
vulvar arch.

13. The whole of the
Heel Stone is visible in
this photograph taken 24
minutes after sunrise on 1
July 1987. Although the day
of the actual Midsummer
Marriage is long past, the
effect of the shadow can
be seen for two weeks after
the solstice, or as early as
two weeks preceding it,
from a position outside
the monument.

14. The bluestones inside the outer vulvar entrance of the sarsen circle emphasise the vaginal approach to the inner womb.

15. The remaining stones of the cove in the northern circle at Avebury henge. The Goddess Stone is on the left and one of her phallic consorts on the right. The midsummer sun rises over Hackpen Hill three kilometres to the north-east beyond the trees.

16. The instant of
midsummer sunrise
when the sun peeks over
Hackpen Hill to produce
the Midsummer Marriage
at the cove. Photographed
15 June 1986.

17. Avebury's Goddess
Stone turns red in the early
morning sunshine, and the
author's shadow, like that of
the phallic shade from stone
F, is cast upon it.
Photographed 15 June
1986

18. Stone 106 at Avebury, with its prominent vulva mark to the ENE, is set facing the early-May sunrise and the missing megalith called The Obelisk. This alignment hints at a Spring Wedding fertility rite, linking female stone, rising sun and shade - the principle of the Sacred Marriage. Stukeley drew the phallic obelisk on 10 July, 1723, writing that it 'is of a circular form at the base, of a vast bulk, 21 feet long, and 3 feet 9 inches diameter when standing, higher than the rest.'

19. Close-up of the vulva mark on Stone 106 in Avebury's southernmost inner circle.

previous occasions, were spaced about in their final order in the middle of the circles. The inner sanctum was crowded with stones and starved of light from the horizons. Although open to the sky, the broad sarsens dimmed the field of vision and created a certain gloom. There were so many stones, bluestones included, that for much of the year light from the rising sun could not get past them. But the light that brought Stonehenge to life suddenly arrived on midsummer morning when the gaps came straight and the sun met the Altar Stone face to face. This central trilithon gap was wider than the rest, purpose-made to let the sun shine through. And yet so quickly afterwards the shutter closed as the eclipse took place and sent piercing shade into the womb that was Stonehenge. The golden orb, rising clear of the Heel Stone on midsummer's day and shining through the central trilithon gap of the sarsen ring, met its Goddess icon in illuminated intercourse before the extinguishing eclipse replaced seminal light with shadowed union. The stone was not only at the Centre of the World, in the usual religious sense, *it was at the centre-back of the womb*. The U-shape arrangement of great trilithons duplicated the human womb, and the Altar Stone was the Womb Stone!

The spectacle was a reminder of the community's origins at the beginning of time, when life began. Of necessity it was transitory and a deeply moving religious experience for the participants. As Mircea Eliade wrote in *The Quest*, this would be a supreme example of 'the profane being transmuted into the sacred by the dialectics of hierophany', that is by the logic of revelation. Just as the belief of the faithful can turn wine into blood, so can similar spiritual logic turn, as here, a stone into a deity.

9

The Marriage is Consummated

It is an epic stage-set. The visual display is exquisitely and sensitively composed, one which every onlooker could appreciate.

The underlying myth is that of the Marriage of the Gods, also known as the divine hierogamy—proof that the architects of Stonehenge believed in the creation myth, at one time so widespread throughout the archaic world, of union between Sky and Earth, or Sun and Moon, or Sky-Father and Great Goddess. It is the classic encounter between complementary opposites meeting in union, that supreme moment at the beginning of time when the world was created.

Hierogamy was a symbolical, dramatic episode in the calendar of agrarian peoples. In so many other cultures of the past, known to us through sagas, poetry, folklore and later historical sources, the Sacred Marriage was a fertility rite, associated with New Year, spring or summer festivals, which involved the ritual mating of people who for the purpose of the ceremony represented the gods. The rite's common, universal objective was to ensure the fertility and productivity of women, animals and crops. In her study of the Neolithic goddesses and gods of south-east Europe Marija Gimbutas discusses the archaeological evidence for fertility worship and provides solid evidence

Artist's impression of the Marriage of the Gods. Stonehenge comes to life at the annual wedding of the Goddess with the Sky God on midsummer day—the only time of the year when the sun's rays and the phallic shadow of the Heel Stone can penetrate the vulvar gate and reach the centre of the womb.

that the principles of ritual Divine Marriage in south-east Europe are unlikely to have commenced later than about 6500 BC.

At Stonehenge we find the Divine Wedding rendered as a dramatic spectacle delicately pictured in timeless stone with the rising sun and moving shade. It is a marriage between images, transfigured and glorified as a marriage between gods.

Every summer on the day when the rising sun arrived at its most northerly point along the horizon the Rite of the Divine Marriage was celebrated as a formal re-enactment of Divine Union. It was solemnly performed in the traditions of the ancestors by an expectant, grateful people wishing to guarantee the safety of their world and the fertility of their crops. Viewed thus, the myth and ritual of the Hierogamy provided a model of their universe. What was for so many archaic societies, elsewhere and in future ages, and not least in south-east Europe, Crete, Greece, and the Middle

East, a priestly rite richly embroidered in myth and ritual, was at Stonehenge transformed into a beauteous vision through the performance of the stones.

In discussing the dramatic viewpoint of early societies Joseph Campbell said that in the theatrical drama-logic of religious festivals the cult object is identifiable at least for the duration of the rites with the divinity.

So it is with Stonehenge.

At the culminating moment, when the sun mates with the Stonehenge Goddess, the Heel Stone eclipses the sun. The shadow crosses the Womb Stone or Goddess Stone (formerly known as the Altar Stone, but which I shall henceforth call by one of these more appropriate names) and completes the consummation of the ritual marriage on the very day that the sun's power is greatest.

But this is no ordinary stone, and certainly not an 'altar stone' either. The receptive stone is tall and graceful; it stands at the centre of the Spiritual World, on the vertical axis that unites Heaven and Earth, and which traverses and sustains the world. In the mythology of the times its shape—the extended rectangle—related as it is to the feminine lozenge, was viewed anthropomorphically because of its links with the form and attraction of the feminine forces of nature. This stone is the core element of the Goddess, a manifestation of the Earth Mother, like the entire construction about her. The stone circles and U-shapes, with medial passage and gaps, represent womb, cervix, vagina and vulva, just as in earlier centuries the white outer bank of Stonehenge (then two metres high) with its stoneless, wooden centre, may have betokened womb or abdominal wall. The correlation is with door/hole symbolism in which the meaning is identical whether between door and hole, or between causewayed-entrance and Womb Stone, or between circumference and centre. All are feminine images and symbols, the door giving access to the hole.

So we can understand why Stonehenge *is what it means*, because Stonehenge stands, in Old English, for stone 'hanging'—that is, stones 'supported in the air'. The 'entry-passage' stones, numbers 1 and 30 in the general plan shown on p. 94), were vested with a hanging stone—the horizontal lintel which completed the trilithon—in order to present the womb-opening as a true hole to guarantee the most effective spectacle. The concept was then continued all round the circle to meet the demands of symmetry and beauty. It is the lintelled sarsens—the hanging stones, their purpose justified by hole symbolism—that make sarsen Stonehenge the unique megalithic spectacle that everyone knows. No other satisfactory explanation for the trilithons of Stonehenge has ever been put forward, and the present answer is now considered to be the correct one. At the same time there is another important feature of the trilithon principle—the statement of the three-stone combination by which is proclaimed the *divine* triplicity of the triple-function goddess. Marija Gimbutas summarises the position of threefold symbolism in *The Language of the Goddess*. She records the antiquity of the triple Goddess principle by its appearance in a Magdalenian context at the Abri du Roc aux

The Heel Stone shadow on 23 June 1988, photographed from directly in front of the Heel Stone a few minutes after the Cosmic Consummation. The phallic shadow is already withdrawing from its union with the Goddess.

Sorciers, Angles-sur-Anglin, France, where there is a relief of three enormous female presences with exposed vulvas. Divine triplicity in one form or another is easily traceable in all prehistoric and classical religions, right through to Irish Newgrange, Celtic triple Brigit, Greek Moirai and Roman triple *Matres* (or *Matronae*).

Viewed as a whole, Stonehenge was not just a temple to the Goddess; it *was* the Goddess, and it remains the ancient Goddess to this day!

And the Heel Stone is phallic after all, which explains why it was set beyond the henge bank, clear of the Goddess's abdomen. The idea was divine coitus *and* impregnation. For as in India, where a tree's shadow was understood to have fertilising powers, so at Stonehenge a similar function was probably assigned to the ejaculating shade of the Heel Stone. This idea is further supported by the phenomenon of detumescence which watchers could contemplate from outside the henge bank. After observing the ritual marriage, first by the sun's rays and then by the conjunction of phallic shade with vaginal entrance in the sarsen wall, worshippers could watch the physical detumescence of the shadow after the wedding. The dramatic spectacle, until then restricted to perhaps a couple of dozen devotees inside the stone circles, could now be seen by hundreds more from without. In fact, those attending outside were treated to an equally stimulating and more prolonged pageant than observers remaining inside. A truly practical purpose for the Heel Stone's sacred circle now becomes evident, because by avoiding the sanctity of the little circle, the watchers and their long shadows would not obstruct the miracle of the shadowgraph.

This magnificent spectacle, the Coitus of the Gods, as viewed from outside the temple, continues to this day. It can be followed by anyone who stands on the path next to where the Heel Stone is situated, and I have studied the phenomenon myself every summer since 1986. In the first minutes after sunrise the mating spectacle is seen—first by the sun's rays and then by the shadow, the shadow entering the middle trilithon archway—after which, for an hour or so, the detumescence can be watched. This central trilithon archway is the only trilithon which lets the light of the nuptial sun reach the Womb Stone; it is the only trilithon arch which lets through the shadow of the Heel Stone; *it is the vulva of the Goddess.* To view the spectacle from outside Stonehenge, one stands with one's back to the sun. Most people who go there in midsummer week stand in the wrong place and look the wrong way, and restrict themselves—unnecessarily—to one day only, 21 June, as though that used to be the only admissible day for celebration.

What are the best days for viewing the shadow part of the spectacle? For people watching from outside the monument the answer is some ten days before and after 21 June—the day most people think of as the longest day, the day when the sun arrives at its most northerly point along the horizon. But in some years 20 or 22 June is as long or longer. Data for 1991 show 21 and 22 June as identical to within a second of time, while for 1992 the 20th and 21st are similarly alike. Neither is there much difference between these three dates for the solar rising position, as the azimuths in Table III confirm. This table also shows that the dates of the earliest rising and the latest setting of the sun (17 and 25 June respectively) are well removed from the date of midsummer's day. For people observing from the Womb Stone at the centre of Stonehenge, although the sun's extreme point of rising to the left of the Heel Stone occurs at the solstice, there is no significant difference between 20 and 22 June, and probably not enough to matter for 19 and 23 June either. Even for 24–25 June (as for 17–18) the difference may not have unduly bothered the gathered assembly if poor weather denied them a viewing opportunity on the best dates; but other dates for this inside-viewing position are not acceptable, because the sun does not rise clear of the Heel Stone before being eclipsed by it. The chief point is that, although 20–22 June is the target period, depending on the weather, the priests or priestesses might have announced the day of the Marriage fertility festival to be nigh on any day from, say, 17 June onwards. Indeed, for all we can tell, the summer festival may have spread over several days. As regards the best period for present-day visitors to watch the

TABLE III

Stonehenge: azimuth, midsummer sunrise and sunset times for a horizon altitude of 0.5°

Date	Azimuth	Sunrise	Sunset	Length of Day
June 15	50.46	3 h 56.16	20 h 19.68	16 h 23.52 min
June 16	50.38	3 h 56.10	20 h 20.14	16 h 24.04 min
June 17	50.32	3 h 56.08	20 h 20.55	16 h 24.47 min
June 18	50.27	3 h 56.12	20 h 20.91	16 h 24.79 min
June 19	50.23	3 h 56.20	20 h 21.23	16 h 25.03 min
June 20	50.211	3 h 56.35	20 h 21.50	16 h 25.15 min
June 21	**50.201**	3 h 56.53	20 h 21.72	**16 h 25.19 min**
June 22	50.205	3 h 56.75	20 h 21.89	16 h 25.14 min
June 23	50.22	3 h 57.01	20 h 22.01	16 h 25.00 min
June 24	50.25	3 h 57.33	20 h 22.08	16 h 24.75 min
June 25	50.29	3 h 57.71	20 h 22.10	16 h 24.39 min
June 26	50.35	3 h 58.12	20 h 22.07	16 h 23.95 min

NOTES: The calculations were done at the author's request by Dr Bernard D. Yallop for June 1989, using the Stonehenge latitude of 51 degrees 11 minutes north, longitude 1 degree 51 minutes west, for apparent horizon altitudes of 0, 0.5, 0.6 and 1.0 degree. Only the figures for 0.5 degree are reproduced here. The exact elevation of the horizon in 2000 BC is uncertain because the extent of tree-cover is not known; an elevation of 0.6 degree may be preferable. Sunrise times refer to the first gleam of the sun, and sunset times to the last gleam. As no allowance has been made for refraction and parallax, the times are to be used only for purposes of intercomparison with one another.

This information is reproduced with permission from data supplied by the Science and Engineering Research Council.

movement of the Heel Stone shadow from outside the monument, there is even more leeway. Although the shadow only penetrates the trilithon womb-opening from 12–30 June, a passable though incomplete impression of the action of the mating shadow can still be gained by attending any of the sunrises from 9 June to 3 July. The drama is at its best, of course, when the sun rises bright and clear in a cloudless sky. The shadows are then sharp and the spectacle sensational.

The statement of symbolical divine marriage, as a re-enactment of the mythical core-element of the dramas of creation of life and the universe, is overwhelming. In so many primitive mythologies there is a quasi-universal theme that, subsequent to the primaeval separation of Heaven and Earth, chaos reigned until cohesion was restored by re-uniting the gods at the beginning of mortal time. The Marriage of the Gods at Stonehenge could be regarded as a living myth, in which the solsticial stage-set combined the community's vivid mythology with the eternal crisis of the renewal of life. If we can judge from what is known of the hierogamy in other agricultural communities, we may understand how these rites concerned people's desires for prosperity by their appeal not only for a regularity of the crop cycle and an abundant harvest but for the fertility of animal stock and the fecundity of humans. That is to say, the rite of Sacred Marriage was an impassioned prayer for the constancy of the cyclic rhythm of existence.

Hence, the Marriage of the Gods made sense of the central mystery that tormented agrarian societies. It provided a rational explanation for the periodical renewal of the world and the harmonious cycle of life, death and rebirth, which embraced planting, seed growth and the birth, death and resurrection of mankind. *Stonehenge was a replica of the universe in microcosm. The midsummer marriage was a repetition of the Creation in an intelligible, memorable and inspiring form.*

And it was the creation of the Stonehenge Cursus that gave birth to the idea; the scheme was to transmute into stone the Consummation of the Cursus.

The Cursus of the Gods was created from the sexual intercourse of the Sky God with the Great Goddess; and Stonehenge was devised to harmonise and function with the cursus. Aubrey Burl pointed out that the circular earthwork of the first Stonehenge was sited fairly centrally on a slope so that the entire cursus could be seen from it; and, as he acknowledged, the sole causeway in the south side of the cursus seems to point back to Stonehenge along the line of sight of midsummer sunrise (in which direction the avenue was to be constructed hundreds of years later). These, among others, can be considered as potential reasons for the choice of site for Stonehenge. At the summer solstice the rising sun shines down the Stonehenge Avenue, uniting Cursus and Henge along open causeways. The divine influence of the Sky God's cursus was directed to the ritual centre of the henge.

We should here recall that the meteorological origin of the Cursus emanated from the potency of the long, dark tornado cloud and its union with Earth. In the choreography of Stonehenge the Heel Stone's long, dark shadow traverses the ground and kisses the Womb Stone of the Goddess. In shape the shadow resembles the spiralling tornado cloud, because it too is long, slender, and cone-shaped. The old, spiralling whirlwind traditions of the fourth-millennium Cursus were carried forth to the third and second millennium Stonehenge—but now the stones provided the conjugal meeting place where the Divine Powers were to serve the needs of the community. The Womb Stone of the Goddess is the key to understanding the agrarian Goddess of the Stonehenge drama. In the stoneless centre of the earlier, simpler henge a totem of wood, or other construction, could have served this purpose, but five hundred years later a replacement was sought in lasting mineral.

If she is Goddess of Earth, then in the mythology of the times she is likely to have been Goddess of the Moon and Heaven as well, and the substantial evidence for lunar observance at the henge is not inconsistent with this. The horned head of the bull, often considered in other well-researched cultures to be an animal manifestation of the Great Goddess (besides, of course, the Sky God), bore lunar rights and qualities through its symbolic resemblance with the horned moon. Although the choreography was different at Knossos, some of the Stonehenge practices or sentiments may have resembled the Cretan rites of Divine Marriage between Zeus and Hera. At Knossos this was celebrated in a mythological framework which A. B. Cook has analysed to show Sun-Bull united with Moon-Cow. The bull-skulls, the horn cores, and the antler horns, deposited in cursus and henge ditches, barrows and henge centres may have had a functional correspondence with the Minoan horns of consecration; they are at any rate clear proof of an Ancient British bull-cult. In fact, in Minoan and Mycenean spiritual belief they were symbols of the Great Goddess, not a patriarchal deity, and in Ancient Britain too there is reason to link the early stage of the bull-cult with matriarchal as well as patriarchal features.

One may add that, of the early cremations deposited in Aubrey Holes, only one (hole 55) had any object interred with it. This hole, which was on a north-east bearing, received two antlers, an offering that would seem to be dedicatory because of its firm fertility overtones aimed at the lunar Goddess. Later, about 2500 BC, part of the ditch near the east side of the causeway was filled with rammed chalk-rubble and the axis of the causeway modified. This signalled that the bluestones and the future Womb Stone of the Goddess were coming to the henge.

10

Goddesses of Stone

The megalith chosen to be the Goddess's Womb Stone at Stonehenge came from the Cosheston rocks of the South Wales coast, and was selected because of its mica content. It would have been erected before its bluestone companions, otherwise it would not have got through the circles planned to surround it. This pale-green mineral with its flakes of mica sparkles in the sunlight when freshly scraped and wetted. Could any knowledge of this, an annual rasping and wetting, have survived as a folk memory from the last days of Stonehenge, around 1000 BC, to the time of Geoffrey of Monmouth, about AD 1138? Geoffrey was the mediaeval historian who wrote of the curative powers of the stones when drenched with water, and, still later, in 1707, the Reverend James Brome reported that 'if the stones be rubbed, or scraped, and water thrown upon the scrapings, they will (some say) heal any green wound, or old sore.'

Aubrey Burl suggests that the Altar Stone (the stone I call the Womb Stone of the Goddess) may have functioned, as in Brittany, as a 'guardian goddess', a protectress of the spirits of the dead, and he suggested that the stone axe found at its base proclaims its role as the 'guardian of the dead'. In Anglesey, at the Goddess temple of Bryn Celli Dhu, the free-standing pillar stone inside the womb-chamber may have functioned as the central Goddess idol. The free-standing white stone in the interior of Cairn L on the Loughcrew Hills in Ireland could have been specially regarded as a Goddess icon too. At Ty-Ar-Boudiquet in Finistère the comparison with Stonehenge is striking. This V-shaped passage grave faces the midwinter sunrise, at which time

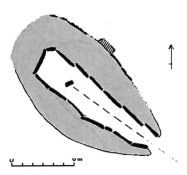

Ty-ar-Boudiquet, one of the Breton sites where the Marriage of the Gods was ritualised in stone. The free-standing megalith in the womb of the Goddess monument receives the seminating sunlight at midwinter, the start of the New Year.

Inside Ty-ar-Boudiquet. Three of the horizontal capstones are missing, and the Goddess Stone can be seen inside, awaiting the midwinter sunrise.

the rising sun enters the chamber and illuminates a free-standing megalith nine metres inside the passage. This stone, which is certainly the local Goddess idol, awaits her annual winter visit from the sun.

At Stonehenge no attempt was made to give the Womb Stone of the Goddess any human-related features. Formless but symbolic, the Stonehenge image was potent and efficient as it was. In any case human indications were inappropriate because the stone was not so much the Goddess as a stone within her womb, albeit the principal stone of the womb. It signified, nevertheless, the cult deity about which the elaborate ritual choreography was devised. Stonehenge was therefore a temple in even the narrowest sense of the definition required by religious historians who hold that a true temple accommodates an icon of the deity about which the cult is centred. At Stonehenge, not only does this apply, but the whole structure was designed to represent the deity.

The Womb Stone of the goddess temple rose about the year 2500 BC, but work on the erection of the bluestone circles in their symbolic womb-pattern, begun at the same time, was never completed. As the bluestones went up, it seems to have been thought that the overall operation was insufficient to realise the potentialities of the site. The work was halted, the bluestones were taken down, and the exercise restarted with the audacious sarsen scheme that is Stonehenge as we know it. For a while the numerous bluestones had to be 'stored' somewhere. Perhaps they were set up as a ring nearby, as Rodney Castleden suggests, but I propose they may have acted as temporary sentinel guards lining the avenue running north-east from Stonehenge. This avenue was built roughly at a time that would make this theory possible. In fact, there is recent evidence by geophysical testing to suggest that stones once followed both sides of the earthen avenue. Whatever happened to the bluestones in between, they eventually reached their final positions lining the Womb of Stonehenge, where they expressed fertility and virility in a pattern of male-type and female-type stones.

Likenesses of Neolithic goddesses in stone or wood are rare in ancient Britain. Few megaliths have been so sculpted on the British mainland. Symbolic representations are more common, as discussed in *The Goddess of the Stones*. In northern France Goddess Stones are more easily recognised because a limited degree of carving was performed on many. Typical from Neolithic Brittany are partly-tooled menhirs with well-developed shoulders and indications of a neck. The standing stones at Medréac exemplify this. On the Isle of Man a splendid stone of this type stands at Cashtal-yn-Ard chambered tomb. We may be sure about the intentions of those who sculpted such works because of numerous anthropomorphic carvings found on tomb-slabs in Brittany where gracefully-chiselled breasts, necklaces and sometimes arms on necked and shouldered outlines were sometimes added. The megalithic engravings at the Allée Couverte of Prajou Menhir (Côte-du-Nord) are distinctive, as are the Déesse Mère statue from the Island of Guernsey and the sculpture from Laniscar (Finistère) which present the theme in three dimensions.

A splendid stone of shining calcite at Medréac in Brittany, the top roughly hewn into the 'head-and-shoulders' so typical of Neolithic Goddess icons in Ancient Gaul. Other megaliths in stone rows nearby show similar treatment.

A carving of four breasts—two small and two big—which may represent the Goddess before and after pregnancy. These are at Prajou Menhir, an *allée couverte* in the Côte du Nord, Brittany, another Goddess monument. Neolithic breast carvings are found at many megalithic tumuli in France.

A Goddess Stone from Laniscar, Finistère, identifiable by its shouldered neck, breasts and necklace.

These carvings are called to mind at Stonehenge by the engraving on the inside of one of the vertical stones of the fourth great trilithon (stone 57). This design has affinities with Goddess representations from Brittany, as Aubrey Burl has strongly advocated, and I agree that it is certainly a Stonehenge Goddess icon. Its simplicity of outline belies the effort that went into executing it, because the large area indicated was wholly hammered out in relief. This elementary piece of art depicting a female deity from the third or second millennium BC was set on the left (that is, to the west) of the Womb Stone. It is possible that on the days when the monument was in use the carving's presence was highlighted by painting it or by marking it out in chalk. There is a second engraving, less clear, on the same surface, and, if Rodney Castleden is correct, another as a rebate on a nearby lintel (stone 120). However, when Mr Castleden's stone rubbing on this lintel is inverted, it resembles instead an incipient tornado funnel cloud, logically located on a stone 'in the sky' on the western side of the monument, the direction in which the cursus-making tornado cloud could have been witnessed a few centuries earlier—and forming part of an epic tale from the days of the ancestors. Unfortunately, the stone has lain on the ground for centuries, and been damaged by the feet of visitors.

Opposite, across the sacred space of the inner sanctum, on the inside face of a

At Stonehenge this outline of a Goddess image is carved in relief on the inside of the western trilithon arch nearest the Goddess Womb Stone (Altar Stone). It measures 1.1 metres high by one metre broad.

trilithon stone to the right of the Womb Stone (that is, to its east), are the well-publicised Bronze-Age dagger carvings. Again, we can agree with Aubrey Burl that they may symbolise the protective abilities of the Great Goddess, so despite being on the right-hand side and of Bronze Age date, they are unlikely to denote the power of some male warrior divinity. A second link with the Goddess is more acceptable because the habitual V-shape of axe and dagger provides an ancient symbolic link with the female triangle and vulva. Like the Breton Goddess whose Goddess stones so often bear axe carvings, the Goddess is here rendered as the Great Protectress.

Stones which are said to exhibit masculine or feminine propensities are commonly encountered in Neolithic and Bronze Age monuments. There are some at Stonehenge. The best surviving pair is positioned just inside the outer sarsen circle on either side of the principal trilithon entrance—the womb-opening of the Goddess—so that the

The dagger carvings on the trilithon stone to the east of the Goddess Womb Stone (Altar Stone). The carvings are about 30 centimetres in length. A photograph of the whole stone is on p. 96.

wedding rays of the rising sun, soon to be supplanted by phallic shade, pass between them at midsummer.

Stones are assigned masculine attributes when they are obviously phallic in shape, or appear so when regarded from the intended viewing direction. Femininity is assigned to broader stones, especially those with rhomboid, rectangular, or lozenge-like characteristics. Many examples are known from Avebury and other ancient centres of worship, including megalithic chambered tombs. The lozenge form which evokes the wide-open vulva is typical of the feminine stones at Avebury.

Sexuality symbolised in stone has been affirmed through drawing unambiguous comparisons with explicit carvings which bear sexual characteristics, or because of obvious fertility associations with stone balls, phalluses, and cups. One of the chalk balls from the Neolithic phase of Stonehenge was found in a deposit in the outer ditch, as was a female cup made from a block of chalk. William Hawley's discovery of a perforated disc and ball in the outer ditch may be similarly explained.

Objects like these have been found at other Neolithic sites. Some well-polished

A lozenge stone twinned with a male stone, one of many such pairs in the Kennet Avenue at Avebury. Photograph taken at midwinter sunset on 22 December 1985.

stone balls from the Grooved Ware period at Skara Brae in the Orkneys bore spiral carvings as a plain indicator of their role in life-producing rituals. William Hawley's chalk ball from Stonehenge lay close to 'the horn-core of a large bovine animal, having the appearance of a bison'. The probability that masculine fertility symbolism was intended is reinforced by Hawley's subsequent finding together of 'a small horn core of a young bison and two roughly round objects of cut chalk, perhaps intended for balls'. Hollow horn cores have been found in use more recently among primitive societies around the world, sometimes functioning as penis protectors at circumcision and other rituals.

In *The Goddess of the Stones* it is explained how the universal symbolism of the lozenge represents the Great Goddess. This comes about as an extension of vulvar symbolism via the principle that the distinctive, essential part stands for the whole. A chalk plaque from a ritual pit at Stonehenge Bottom carries a repetitive multi-lozenge pattern which strikingly resembles a similarly engraved stone from the Grooved Ware village of Skara Brae in the Orkneys.

Two tablets carved from chalk, found in a ritual pit close to Stonehenge. In different ways both patterns express vulvar symbolism. Because every trilithon, real or drawn, can now be recognised as a Goddess symbol, opposed triple trilithons produce an even more potent vulvar image, as on the left tablet, particularly the middle pair. The second tablet conveys the same message by diagonal grooves which criss-cross to create Goddess lozenges similar to those found in Scottish and Irish tumuli. These are plainly sacred tablets of a Goddess-worshipping society.

Sacred Goddess lozenges and grooves inscribed on the smooth face of a stone tablet from Skara Brae in the Orkneys.

On stone 3 at Stonehenge, 25 cm above the turf-line in a middle position, is the outline of a lozenge whose vertical diagonal measures 111 mm. A smaller one is close by. These are the marks to which Richard Atkinson referred in 1979 when he recorded 'a trellis or lattice pattern . . . low down . . . of a kind similar to some of the geometric patterns executed on the kerb-stones of . . . New Grange in Ireland'. The marks, which may or may not be artificial, are best seen when the sun is in the east. They would have been observed, if not made, by the Stonehenge people who dressed the stone, and were left there for the Goddess symbols which they are. Lost since Atkinson reported them, the author found them on 31 August 1996 at 7 a.m. They are easier to see than the three axe carvings on the same stone. As suggested for the Goddess markings on stone 57, the presence of the lozenges might at times have been heightened by outlining them in chalk. At first the lozenge symbol seems to have expressed, either chiefly or entirely, the fertility aspirations of the artist and worshipper; later it came to symbolise the Goddess. In a still later epoch the meaning broadened and the lozenge came to stand for any divinity, male or female, until it was eventually taken over in the Christian era and used in art, sculpture and painting as a celestial designation for Christ himself.

Among the gold regalia retrieved from the rich burial of a chieftain in the round barrow near Stonehenge known as Bush Barrow were two splendid gold objects delicately inscribed with repeating lozenge patterns. This barrow is part of a cemetery on Normanton Down, in full view of Stonehenge two kilometres away. Whatever purpose the objects served, the patterning is typical of the Neolithic and Bronze Age periods and tells us that the deceased person in Bush Barrow held an eminent post in sacred or high office in a Goddess-based religion, the religion of sarsen Stonehenge at the time of its construction.

At various times additional stones have stood in the region of the main causewayed entrance to Stonehenge. This is known from the discovery of vacant stone-holes during the 1922 excavations of William Hawley, and the 1979 discovery by Michael Pitts of a stone-hole NNW of the Heel Stone. There is also John Aubrey's plan of the monument which shows three sarsens nearer to the circles than the Heel Stone. The one surviving stone, fallen and misshapen, is a dressed stone which in the eighteenth century acquired the undeserved title of 'Slaughter Stone'.

Whatever purpose this stone served, there is little doubt that it fell in antiquity. Certainly, the 1922 excavator of this part of Stonehenge, William Hawley, thought it did. This means that the stone either fell accidentally some time during the Early Bronze Age, or was pushed over as no longer required; and that in what may have been a more dissolute interlude than the earlier enthusiastic stone-raising phase, instead of removing it, an attempt was made to dispose of the unwanted stone by sinking it into a long pit. Otherwise, the great effort that was expended burying it has never been satisfactorily explained. In any event, we shall see that *the effect of the presence*

Besides its three axe carvings, stone 3 at Stonehenge has one large and one small lozenge, in the centre near the base.

or absence of the Slaughter Stone as regards the basic enactment of Sacred Marriage between Sun and Goddess makes no difference. The drama of the annual marriage takes place just the same, as it will forever into the future. For this is indisputably the primary purpose of sarsen Stonehenge—the performance of a well-loved agricultural fertility rite that may even have risen to the status of a regal-divine mating ceremony.

In 1992, in the journal *Antiquity*, Aubrey Burl tried to show that the Slaughter Stone was levelled in the sixteenth or seventeenth century. He cited an illustration, discussed by Dr Jan Albert Bakker in 1979, which is an engraver's copy initialled R.F. and dated 1575, of a lost sketch of 1568–9 by Lucas de Heere, as evidence that the stone was standing then. The sketch shows what may or may not be the Slaughter Stone (for the stone is portrayed as a boulder and not the dressed tabular slab that it is) near

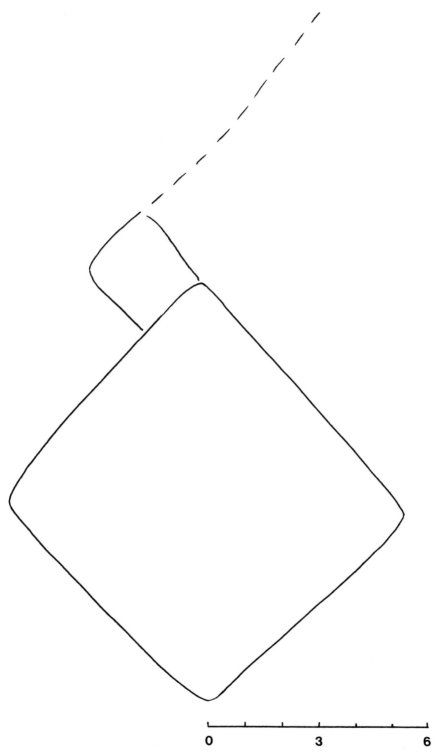

0			3				6

Full-scale reproduction of the lozenge motif on stone 3. The scale is in centimetres.
Symbologists experienced in interpreting primitive feminine imagery recognise this as a
Goddess motif via the principle of the wide-open vulva. Its position at the centre base of the
megalith raises the status of stone 3 to that of a Goddess Stone, possibly linked to the moon
at its most northerly rising (the moon gets eclipsed by the Heel Stone) and the sun at its
midwinter rising.

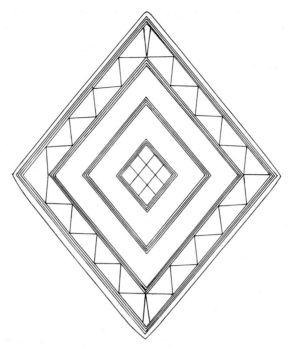

A well-patterned array of Goddess lozenges decorating a gold object 180 millimetres long—
the accompaniment of a rich burial beneath Bush Barrow, a bowl barrow near Stonehenge.

the entrance within the bank a few metres from a second stone; yet the horizontal
dimension of the former is measurably double its vertical dimension, which implies
it was prone, not upstanding. In 1994 Dr Burl sought help from the still later, quite
valueless engraving of Camden which is visibly false in many testable details. It is
easy to see that the latter was a distortion of the 1575 engraving, by a reckless engraver
who redrew every stone, added more, and made others straight including the putative
Slaughter Stone. In fact a well-executed watercolour by de Heere, without entrance
stones, does survive, and this is likely to be similar to the inferred missing sketch
from which R. F. took his engraving.

*But the crucial and convincing proof that the Slaughter Stone lay on its back when
sightseers were at Stonehenge early in the seventeenth century comes from the correct
measurement of its length made soon after 1620,* when King James I asked Inigo
Jones, Surveyor to the Crown, to 'learn what he could of the monument'. In Inigo
Jones's book the stone's length is given as 20 feet, and if it is measured today along
its middle line one finds it is that, to within two inches (5 cm). Jones's measurement

would not have been accurate if the stone had been upright with an unknown quarter or more of its length hidden in the chalk, as are most of the uprights at Stonehenge. Moreover, Jones describes the stone inexactly as 'three foot thick'. This must be because so much of the thickness was out of view below ground that he made a guess by looking at other stones, or else probed for it. Following the archaeological excavations of 1802 and 1920, $1\frac{1}{2}$ feet of the thickness are exposed, and Dr Burl himself writes that the thickness is 0.8m (2ft $7\frac{1}{2}$ins), similar to the 2 feet 9 inches indicated by Cunnington.

Lucas de Heere most likely saw the Slaughter Stone as it is now—huge, recumbent, partly buried, and lying across its stone hole whose depth remains to be ascertained. In any case, no credible motive can be advanced to explain why a sixteenth-century visitor would spend days chiselling out a vast trench in the chalk for the purpose of hiding this stone, whereas there is excellent motivation for a team of Bronze Age worshippers to do just that because the toppling of the megalith possibly represented the termination of an abandoned experiment.

In short, the present evidence implies that for much of the period of use of Stonehenge, from its founding around 3000 BC onwards, no Slaughter Stone was standing, during which time the shadow of the Heel Stone freely reached the unobstructed Goddess Stone inside the stone womb. Unluckily for the worshippers, the weather of the late third and the whole of the second millennium BC was worsening. Research by climatologists informs us that summers were getting cloudier and wetter, and clear sunrises less frequent. The Slaughter Stone's bulk, on a line between the Heel Stone and the Vulva Stones (stones 1 and 30) could be construed as a late attempt to intensify the shadow penetrating the womb. If a quarter of its length was in the chalk, the above-ground height (about 4.5 metres) of the Slaughter Stone was less than that of the then-vertical Heel Stone (5.2 metres). Being nearer to the circles, it would have blocked the Heel Stone for anyone viewing from the centre of Stonehenge, while yet allowing the light of the rising sun to pass. Every year, the predictable sun kept its midsummer appointment. It rose for coitus with the Womb Stone and promptly disappeared behind the Heel Stone, *or behind the combination of Heel Stone and Slaughter Stone*, to dispatch a zone of shade into the womb and extinguish the scintillating light from the base of the sunlit Womb Stone.

Then, for whatever reason, a decision was made to eject the Slaughter Stone, so it was tipped into a coffin-shaped pit to avoid the greater labour of bearing it away. Once more, the Heel Stone became the sole eclipsing agent, timed to follow the mating of Sun with Earth which was the classic norm for thousands of solar-orientated monuments elsewhere. *One must again stress that the question of the Slaughter Stone, and what was or was not apparent in Tudor engravings, has no consequence for the reality or otherwise of the Sacred Marriage ritual.* The sun was there every midsummer morning to penetrate the openings between the stones and reach the gleaming mica-filled Welsh stone waiting in the womb, until stopped by the eclipsing stone whose shadow arrived instead.

Following Michael Pitts's discovery of a big stone-hole north-west of the Heel Stone, it was suggested that the Heel Stone had a companion for a while. This may be so, in which case the rays of the midsummer sun passed between the two stones, although to judge by the location of the extra hole the stones were offset and at differing distances from the circles. The other hole may instead have been a trial hole which temporarily held the Heel Stone in times long before the building of the stone circles. *But when the optimum position was reached the Heel Stone was given its own sacred circle to demonstrate and augment its manifest importance in a stand-alone situation.*

Some people have suggested that at what would be a later stage in the history of Sacred Marriage at Stonehenge a pair of 'portal stones' may have been tried inside the north-east entrance. A hole two metres deep, called Stone Hole E, is close to the Slaughter Stone and a pair could have stood there together, although as Hawley proposed it is possible that the Slaughter Stone occupied Hole E before it fell (in which case it never blocked the line of sight from Heel Stone to Womb Stone). Both Inigo Jones and John Aubrey recorded stones inside the entrance causeway plus one or two others besides, but these men's plans were reconstructions of the damaged monument so one cannot be sure which stones were seen standing or lying. Hawley emphasised that excavation revealed no trace of the four stones mentioned by Inigo Jones at the entrance 'and had they existed as ancient stones the hole would certainly have been found'. He then suggested that to ensure a safe road in muddy conditions for the joyless work of dedicated stone robbers 'four fallen stones might have been taken from the monument and placed there to mark firm ground but not being placed in holes they gradually disappeared'. In truth, Jones indicated twelve stones on his plan, set in fours for the sake of symmetry at three hypothetical entrances, so he may have selected four stones instead of the three that Aubrey saw out of symmetry. Hawley could be partly or wholly right. If de Heere's sketch of 1568–9 is correct in showing two stones in place, the number had increased to three by Aubrey's time.

De Heere's drawing of Stonehenge, done on the spot, was accurate except for the encircling ditch and entrance stones which are shown so incorrectly as to suggest that the artist inserted them from memory. This explains why the ditch has a farcical diameter and the two stones by the entrance are depicted as shapeless boulders, although we know that one (the recumbent Slaughter Stone) was a tooled tabular slab. With such doubts, even its companion (if regarded as Stone E) could have been missing, in which case de Heere's second stone might have been the adjacent Stone D; for Hawley made the astute remark that Stone E must have vanished before Stone D because the crushed sides of Hole D show that the latter was extracted brutally in the direction of Stone E which could not then have been present. Furthermore, lying at the base of Hole E against its sides Hawley found two antlers for which in 1995 Rosemary Cleal and her colleagues reported different ages within the time-span 2480–2200 BC. Their age difference signifies reverential long-term safekeeping—a known mystical feature of the Stone Age. It adds to uncertainty about the time of their deposition which could have been significantly later than 2200 BC, because it is further reported that when six structured deposits of bone material from the great circular ditch were radiocarbon-dated, they were found to be between some 50 and 850 years older than the digging of the ditch! A further possibility is that the antlers from Hole E were ritually inserted into the empty hole after removal of the stone in antiquity; otherwise, if stone-robbers had forcibly extracted Stone E in the Tudor era, the antlers by then 4,000 years old, might have been damaged if not crushed.

It was in 1666 that John Aubrey recorded three stones at the entrance to Stonehenge. One was the half-buried Slaughter Stone, the second was Stone E or D. The third may have been a seventeenth-century addition, as Hawley suggested, or the stone which occupied Hole C. The shallowness of this hole suggests that Stone C was small, while its axial position implies that it pointed to midsummer sunrise for the middle of the third millennium, the time of the main building phase around 2500–2200 BC. If so, Stone B, whose direction from the centre of Stonehenge was slightly farther to the north, could have been put to use in a still earlier age, say 3000 BC, when midsummer sunrise was in that direction. It seems likely that Stone B was taken down, as being in the way, when work on the Avenue began and the sarsens started arriving. Upon completion of the circles the pointer stone was restored, but because the inclination of the ecliptic and the sunrise azimuth had shifted, the opportunity was taken to correct its alignment. The stone was therefore planted at C, and at some later date it came down, but at no time could it have interfered with the light of the sun reaching the centre of Stonehenge because it could not have protruded above the horizon as the much bigger Heel Stone did.

A century ago Mr E. Barclay inferred that the 'Hele Stone' was so called because it was a 'Covering Stone' which he deduced via the Anglo-Saxon word 'helan', meaning to hide or conceal, 'because its shadow covers the [recumbent] sacrificial stone, or slaughter stone, as the sun rises on midsummer morning'. Yes, but before then, before the Slaughter Stone arrived, it was the Goddess Stone or Womb Stone in the centre of the circles which was 'covered'.

A better, more recent suggestion has come from the author's correspondent Mr E. R. Rees of Porthcawl in South Wales. He wondered whether the alternative name for Heel Stone, 'the Friar's Heel', arose from 'Freya's He-ol', Freya being the ancient British/Nordic Goddess and 'he-ol' old Welsh for track or way. This supposes that the Freya He-ol Stone was erected alongside the straight track which is the Stonehenge Avenue. In the seventeenth century John Aubrey was told that the Friar's Heel was a different stone from this, on the west side of the monument (the fallen Stone 14) which bears a heel mark. However, the imprint is more like a complete foot; his informant may therefore have ill-remembered a more ancient tradition relating to the north-eastern, outlying Sun Stone we now call the Heel Stone.

The 'face' that is plainly discernible in the Heel Stone deserves to be mentioned, for it is something about which most writers on Stonehenge say nothing, the tacit assumption being that its presence is accidental. What is more likely is that the people noted a chance facial resemblance, following which a slight improvement to some particular feature was made, for one cannot deny that the 'face' looks equally good when seen from either side.

Lastly, some people may claim that the Heel Stone was not set up until around 2500 BC, about the time that the great sarsens arrived (using the latest dating evidence reported by Cleal *et al.* in 1995). If this proves true, it is important to know that it will not affect the essential theory relating to the coitus of Sun with Goddess; one might then view the positioning of the phallic Heel Stone as the increased masculinis-ation of the cult and monument by newly-arrived axe-wielding Indo-Europeans. It is not impossible that at Stonehenge, as in the Sumerian cities of Ur and Isin in the same epoch, the Sacred Marriage theme was taken to its logical limit by introducing ceremonial copulation. We know that in Sumer the king identified himself as the husband of the Goddess Inanna and, for the good of the fertility and prosperity of his land and people, fornicated ritually with a priestess of Uruk who served as surrogate for Inanna. A script, with choral responses, of part of the ceremony survives, and its vigorous erotic poetry rich with sexual innuendo and euphemism convincingly demonstrates the dramatic strength of the love-making ceremony and masque.

Some writers, the latest being John North in 1996, claim that the primary objective of Stonehenge was to watch the sun setting in the south-west at the midwinter solstice; and that nobody waited at the centre because the chief objective was to have people standing by the Heel Stone to see the midwinter sun set through the arch of the great trilithon. Such writers have no feeling for the finesse of the symbolism with which the stones were endowed, and the sophistication behind the intelligent planning which produced a Goddess temple with sensitive womb directed towards the north-eastern causeway, the Heel Stone, Avenue and midsummer rising sun. The midwinter argu-ment does not allow for the fact that the vertical Goddess Stone, or 'Altar Stone', would have blocked the view and prevented anyone who was standing by the Heel Stone from witnessing a winter solsticial sunset.

Certainly, this converse alignment exists, and one may justifiably assume that calendrical if not ritual advantage was taken of it. The midwinter setting sun shines through the arch of the great trilithon and would have illuminated the reverse side of the upright Goddess Stone, showing that the shortest day was nigh and the momentous New Year's celebrations could commence. Nevertheless, Sarsen Stonehenge was built primarily to honour the midsummer solstice, when Sun met Womb and Goddess Stone front to front. In other parts of Britain, not least the Stonehenge region, many constructions were directed at the winter solstice; these were New Year monuments, but at Stonehenge the importance of the Winter Solstice celebrations was secondary to the grand midsummer fertility festival.

The symbolic image behind the iconography of Stonehenge through its rite of the Marriage of the Gods can be regarded as an integration of the sexes. It signifies the generating power of the universe in the absence of which continuous creation would stop. Such images have occupied the minds of farming peoples from the most ancient of days to the most recent of centuries, and an accessible and rich supply can be found in the mythologies of the American Indians. A petroglyph from Spook's Canyon, California, graphically portrays the Sun mating with the Earth Mother, her womb symbolised by a complex labyrinth. Such imagery recalls the spiritual significance of solar-orientated long barrows in Britain. So many of these fourth-millennium constructions face directions between south-east and north-east that they, too, strongly suggest a Divine Marriage between the rays of the rising sun and the Earth Mother's womb. The forecourt entrance to the chambered barrow or passage grave is modelled on the womb-opening which leads to a vault or chamber, the place of rebirth or regeneration for the souls of the dead. Among the many dozens of tumuli to which this could apply there is the well-known Stoney Littleton (which faces south-east), Newgrange (south-east), East Kennet (south-east), Wayland's Smithy (south-east), Hetty Pegler's Tump (east-south-east), West Kennet (east), Knowth (east), Nympsfield (east), Bryn Celli Dhu (north-east), and Avening Court (north-east). A few, like Dowth at midwinter and Cashtal-yn-Ard at the equinox, have sunset alignments instead.

A rock carving from Spook's Canyon in southern California showing the sun's rays entering the Earth Mother's labyrinth at the time of the wedding of the Sky God with the Goddess.

Another American Indian rock carving is a vivid creation petroglyph from the Iroquois of Tennessee. Here the Sun God's penis and Earth Mother's vulva are accompanied by an abstract symbol meaning 'to do' or 'to make', which adds power to the symbolic insemination. The Earth Mother's womb, represented by a five-fold spiral, was described by the Potowatomi medicine-priest interpreter as a 'coiled serpent or labyrinth symbol expressing the idea that children or young exist in the womb-world fastened together as on a vine or cord'. The Earth Mother's 'Vine of Progeny' issues from the womb and loops back to the phallus and vulva, completing an endless cycle of creation. The whole is watched over by the guardian or priest. It is remarkable how the primary elements of this composition—penis, vulva and womb—apply with unexpected perfection to Stonehenge.

The Origin of Life, depicted in an American Indian petroglyph from Tennessee. The elements are (1) the Sun God's phallus; (2) the Earth Goddess's vulva; (3) the verb *to do* or *to make*; (4) the Goddess's womb of generation, and (5) the subsequent offspring (the Vine of Progeny). Located in the corner on the left is the spiritual guardian.

Both these stone carvings would have been understood without difficulty by the symbol-makers of the Age of Stonehenge. In both, as in the mural from Neolithic Dorchester (see p. 45), we are in the magical world of Divine Marriage by means of the symbolism of sexual union. In America it is the picture symbolism of a recent Neolithic age; at Dorchester the picture symbolism dates broadly from the same time period as the earliest phase of Stonehenge, when ditch and bank were constructed and the destiny of the Heel Stone was decreed.

Whatever the situation may have been at that time in the third millennium, there was a later tendency throughout Europe for the dominion of early agrarian Great Goddesses to be reduced by the rising power of Sky Gods. They began as simple consorts, but increasingly tended to become potential, usurping warrior gods. The Beaker-using peoples may have assisted in spreading such changes, and indeed, the replanning of Stonehenge from 2500 BC onwards was the work of British Beaker forces and their descendants. If so, the thematic problem at Stonehenge may have been overcome by deifying the ancient Heel Stone as a Sun Stone, so that its powers might be wholly attributable to the work of the sun god. This deification would justify the cutting of the sacred ring about the stone instead of, or as well as, the previous suggestion that the ring kept the multitude from crowding too near the stone on mid-summer's morning. Still later, even more sweeping changes were ruthlessly delivered, for the Late Bronze Age must have seen the complete annihilation of the priests and believers at Stonehenge by unnameable conquerors. Nothing less could account for the abandonment of such a well-loved, precious monument and the ending of the age-old Divine Marriage ceremonies.

Be that as it may, the sarsen phase of Stonehenge rose in the Late Neolithic and Early Bronze Ages at the hands of a race whose leaders appreciated luxury items of gold and bronze. They were the builders of the thousands of round barrows which cover the plains to this day; they were the men and women who inherited beliefs and a tradition which at least in the beginning embraced the divine phenomenon of the tornadic-whirlwind spirit. In the temperament of the age their homes were round dwellings, shaped like their tombs and henges, every one a microcosm of the circular universe, every one a sacred retreat with its own centre.

Their public spiritual centre was the circular temple of Stonehenge whose cyclopean construction was taken to completion because of the force and logic of a compelling religious theme. Its over-ambitious design and centuries-long construction and reconstruction could only have been realised by the exercise of an authoritative priestcraft which held the confidence of a powerful ruling class. Stonehenge was not the achievement of a world of shamans whose individualistic talents and use of magical powers belonged to the nomadic groups of northern Europe. The settling of communities and the spread of religious sites permitted priest-led organisations to develop, and Stonehenge was conspicuously the nucleus of the finest of these. The circles were constructed to manifest a people's sacred mythological beliefs by employing a principle which focused on a belief in Divine Marriage. The solemn rituals were re-enacted yearly, at the time of a summer festival, in a vivid and comprehensible form, and with a brilliance, beauty and emotion which modern peoples cannot appreciate.

Nor was this the only British temple at which the Marriage of the Gods was so grandly celebrated. Not far north of Stonehenge is another colossus, the megalithic temples at Avebury.

11

The Goddess at Avebury

Avebury is the giant of the world's stone circles.

Stonehenge has the advantage in subtlety of planning and brilliance of execution, but Avebury cannot be matched for its immensity. At the height of its glory a ring of 98 megaliths lined the interior of a henge ditch which was cut over nine metres deep into the chalk rock and had a bank of similar volume outside it. There were four entrance causeways, and, inside, two additional megalithic circle complexes. The southern circle system was centred about a tall stone which William Stukeley learnt was called The Obelisk. Like so many of Avebury's important stones, it is no more, destroyed in one of the fanatical anti-heritage outbursts with which prehistoric Avebury had to contend.

At the centre of the northern circle were three megaliths in a special arrangement known as a cove. This word was introduced by Stukeley to denote a setting of three standing stones, close to one another but not touching, which he described as 'set upon the ark of a circle, regarding each other with an obtuse angle'. Since the time of John Aubrey and William Stukeley, who were the first antiquarians to describe the megalithic coves of ancient Britain, their purpose within the sphere of prehistoric religious ritual has remained a mystery, save for Stukeley's speculation that they were 'perhaps . . . intended . . . for a nich-like hemispherical figure, in some sort to represent the heavens . . . The altar properly lay upon the ground before this superb nich'. As there is no excavation evidence for a missing altar stone, no megalith at Avebury has suffered the misnomer that has blighted terminology at Stonehenge.

The remains of two coves at Avebury survive to this day. Besides the one in the northern circle system, another, known as Beckhampton Cove, is to be found well to the west of the Avebury henge and circles, at a point along the great megalithic avenue called Beckhampton Avenue. By making use of the testimony and drawings of John Aubrey and William Stukeley there is no difficulty in compiling details of the positions and shapes of the cove's missing sarsens.

William Stukeley visited Avebury several times in the years to 1724. His drawing of the cove depicts the three stones D, B and A, and their positions on the northern side of the Beckhampton stone avenue relative to a fourth stone C located on the opposite side of the avenue. Stukeley remarked that one of the avenue stones (stone B) makes the back of the cove but it had toppled backwards. He also learnt that stones D and C had been 'carried off by that destroyer Richard Fowler' seven years earlier. Today only stone A survives, together with stone E, the last avenue stone remaining upright. Fortunately, this is enough to show that stone A stood at an obtuse angle of 110° to the missing back stone, which corresponds well enough with the situation as known for the North Circle Cove. Moreover, as far as one can tell, the back stone formerly faced the local midwinter sunrise, which is close to 130°.

The stones west of Avebury known as the Beckhampton Cove according to the reconstruction by William Stukeley in 1724. Stone A of the cove and stone E of the avenue, which survive to this day, go under the names Adam and Eve. At the time of Stukeley's drawing stone B lay on its back, and a number of other megaliths labelled F lay fallen too. Stones C and D had recently been destroyed.

Stone A, the only surviving megalith of the Beckhampton Cove. It was one of a pair which stood either side of the Goddess Stone (stone B). Viewed from the direction of midwinter sunrise the shape of this broad massive stone becomes narrow and phallic.

The cove is plainly another sacred construction.

The three cove-stones, and stone C facing them, appear to have obvious sexual qualities associated with the essentials either of masculinity (stones D, A and C) or of femininity (stone B). The surviving stone A, seen from the direction which emphasises its intended sexuality, is plainly phallic.

The inclusion of the male cove-stone A, which can be seen in William Stukeley's sketch, is crucial if we are to discover the reasoning behind the cove's construction, because by facing the female cove-stone B, stones C and B worked together as a Divine Marriage pair. Significantly, they were set on a common axis which seems to have been aligned on midwinter sunrise.

The local direction for the solsticial sunrise would be 128.4° for a distant level horizon, but because there is a nearby hill only three hundred metres to the south-east of Beckhampton Cove, which has an elevation of 1.4°, the time of local sunrise is delayed until the sun's azimuth swings to 130.5°.

Because sunrise is delayed by some ten minutes, when the sun does come into sight the power of its rays has increased so much that, as it comes over the hill, it soon

Neolithic and Bronze Age remains in the vicinity of Avebury. Note particularly the relationship between Beckhampton Cove and the midwinter sunrise over the hill to the south-east. If the cove was set on a pre-existing megalithic avenue, the choice of position can be explained by the criterion that the hill would delay the sunrise sufficiently to ensure that it was a bright sun which would come over the hillcrest to mate with the Goddess Stone B. © *Crown copyright.*

shines brightly on the pointed stone C, throwing its shadow directly on to the central cove stone (B). This carefully-planned orientation has immense implications for the purpose of stone C, because its status is raised enormously beyond that of a simple avenue stone. Stone C has to be reckoned as a functional part of the cove.

All priority was given, it seems, to seeking some presumably beneficial effect from having the cove on the avenue. If the latter was indeed the stone-lined equivalent of the ditch-and-bank cursuses of other communities as suggested in Chapter 5, then the concept of Divine Union or hierogamy with the Sky God was already instilled into the sacredness of the stone avenue.

The cove's objective was therefore to welcome and direct the New Year's sun into the avenue-cursus of a Goddess-believing community, a society familiar with the expression of the concept of the Marriage of the Gods through cursus-god beliefs. On midwinter's day the rising sun mated with the Goddess Stone via the direct light of its rays and then, as at Stonehenge, united male and female megaliths with the fertilising power of the shade projected by the intromission of stone C.

So at Avebury Divine Marriage is the theme, just as it is at Stonehenge. The one-time union of the gods, commemorated by the construction of the avenue-cursus, was exalted in a new kind of structure that repeated the mystical event year after year. The cove re-enacted the Cosmic Marriage on midwinter's morning—New Year's Day in those olden times—a ceremonial occasion doubtless accompanied by a winter festival. The same element of astrobiology is present in the religion of both societies, high proof of the importance in their mythologies of sexual union between Goddess and God.

The symbolism is the regeneration of life. At the centre of the cove is the Goddess Stone (B) flanked by male consorts (stones A and D). At Beckhampton Goddess appears as bestower and regainer of life. The triumphant beginning of the New Year brings satisfaction and renewed hope to the uncertain world of the primitive British farmer.

The second cove, inside the northern circle of the Avebury henge, has two stones remaining. This cove was built to stand at the centre of a megalithic circle, but most of its stones are missing. As William Stukeley remarked of the cove: 'It opens pretty exactly north-east, as at Stonehenge', which means, of course, in the direction of midsummer sunrise.

The survivors of the North Circle cove are arguably Avebury's finest stones. Their sexual characters are obvious. The central stone has the typical qualities of female-type megaliths. Viewed from the direction of midsummer sunrise, it displays a polygonal earthbound solidity and massiveness four metres high, which totally contrasts with the slender phallic shape of its taller companion. As for the missing third stone which fell in 1713, William Stukeley was informed by the locals that 'it was full seven yards long, of the same shape as its opposite, tall and narrow'. Thus, viewed from the front, the direction of midsummer sunrise, the middle stone is solidly feminine, its companions wholly masculine. It is indisputable that the shapes of these magnificent stones conveyed an impression of divine sexuality to the informed adorants of the age.

Again we are in the province of the Great Goddess and Earth Goddess. The cove comprised a massive Goddess Stone whose strength was augmented by the masculinity of her two consorts. She awaited the midsummer sunrise in the same fashion that her counterpart at Beckhampton awaited the winter solstice. Was she, too, served by the seed of an eclipsing stone's shadow? If so, this would provide the ultimate realisation of her manifold creative powers.

The answer is positive because it can be shown that a stone was once suitably positioned 22 metres to the north-east. Both Aubrey and Stukeley saw such a stone, a menhir labelled 'F' on Stukeley's plan, at some distance in front of the cove. On Isobel Smith's plan in *Windmill Hill and Avebury* the stone's orientation relative to the cove centre measures about 50° 00′, which is the direction of midsummer sunrise when the sun climbs over Hackpen Hill four kilometres distant. William Stukeley

A drawing of the Avebury Cove made by William Stukeley in 1723, looking south-west from a position next to a fourth cove stone known as Stone F. Stukeley has sketched in the position of the recently-removed third stone.

showed the stone relative to the cove-stones in three of his sketches, as did Mr J. Browne of Avebury in a watercolour which he painted in 1825, three years before the stone's destruction by gunpowder.

The contribution of the fourth stone completes the scene of Divine Marriage at the cove. The stone's position, at 22 metres in front of the Goddess Stone, was placed so that it would eclipse the sun and provide a consummating shadow for the Goddess.

What is more, the summit of stone F does not appear to have been centred precisely opposite the middle stone of the cove, but just a little towards the east, much as the Heel Stone at Stonehenge is positioned slightly to the east of the midsummer-sunrise direction in order to ensure that after solar impregnation the eclipse trick works. Consequently, as at the Beckhampton Cove where cosmic intercourse takes place in midwinter, there is here, in the heart of Avebury, ample proof of a four-stone cove, in which the fourth stone completes the celestial intercourse with the Temple Goddess on midsummer's morning.

On 15 June 1986 I witnessed a perfect midsummer sunrise at the cove. This date is only six days before the sun arrives at its most northerly position along the eastern

The section of the great plan of Avebury drawn by William Stukeley, in which the relative positions of the cove stones including Stone F are shown.

horizon, the true midsummer morning of 21 June. The sun climbed over Hackpen Hill at 0407 GMT (0507 British Summer Time) which is about nine minutes later than it does at Stonehenge on account of the height of the hill. The eclipsing stone, had it been there, would not at first have interfered with the sunrise as viewed from the cove. As at Stonehenge, the sun rose unimpeded to the left of the estimated position of the 'sun stone', and illuminated the Goddess Stone with its rays, suffusing it with the sun's energy and light. But very soon the sun was eclipsed as it passed behind the phallic stone, and for some minutes the Temple Goddess, having initially received the sun's devotion, would have enjoyed the shadow's caress. About 0412 I took an unusual shadow photograph. Standing five metres in front of the Goddess, my shadow had a greenish hue, coloured by the lichen on the otherwise sun-reddened Goddess Stone.

The religious symbolism at Avebury's Cove is clear. The cove was the repository of the power of the Divine—and by consequence that of the priestesses and priests. The vision of the Divine Marriage procured and intensified the belief of the people. On account of its position at the heart of the temple, this splendid stone—a transmutation of the Goddess who on this day appeared in her guise as the Womb Stone and was impregnated in parallel with similar events at Stonehenge no more than thirty kilometres to the south—must have been the most important stone at Avebury. Indeed it is almost the biggest-known stone idol to the Goddess raised in antiquity in Britain, and much more massive than the Womb Stone of the Goddess at Stonehenge. And, as with the Stonehenge Womb Stone, at times of high ceremonial the imagery becomes absolute, because the stone, then fully occupied by the soul and spirit of the Goddess, *is* the Goddess. As inheritors of the prehistoric landscape we are fortunate that this stone, more than any other at Avebury, has endured the attacks of discrimination and violence. This central megalith is as indispensable for a proper understanding of Avebury as is the Goddess's Womb Stone at Stonehenge, because both are Goddess Stones and the stones of Avebury's North Circle may be likened to a womb circle like the U-shaped womb at Stonehenge.

At times of prayer or festival, in addition to the summer solstice, the Goddess might repossess and occupy the stone. Whatever the doctrine or method, whatever the mythological reasoning, the North Circle Cove was her shrine and residence. She was there to offer, as does a church, relief and refuge to believers. At the summer solstice she was sought after and supplicated for her powers of controlling the fertility of the crops, to enrich the harvest and secure the health of animals and people. At Beck-hampton Cove it was the winter solstice that was celebrated, as an insurance for the renewal of the world and the fertility of women and animals as the New Year arrived. The coves were holy places, the foremost shrines of the Windmill Hill people.

The heart of Avebury is like the womb of Stonehenge: both monuments preserve omnipotent icons. The presumption would be that, as in India today, supplication attracts the celestial and earthly deities with the purpose of impregnating the cult images with their holiness. The idea of divine sexual union with phallus and vulva, or *lingam* and *yoni*, united stands for the driving force which runs the world. The Goddess cult reached India in Neolithic times as an eastward extension from the Near East and Europe.

From what we can tell, Neolithic India bore similarities with Neolithic Britain and Ireland, to which the farming immigrants coming from the Continent carried the cult of the agrarian goddess and the theory of the Marriage of the Gods, except that the cursus of the gods was a regional development peculiar to Britain, which at Beckhampton-Avebury was rendered in stone. Not long afterwards work began on Avebury's great rings at the eastern extremity of the earliest stone avenue, and later still the second stone avenue was added as a link to the ancient site on Overton Down which is known as The Sanctuary.

Before we leave Avebury, there is a third Sacred Marriage spectacle to describe. This one took place inside the southernmost inner circle and was timed for May Day, the fertility festival known later as Beltane.

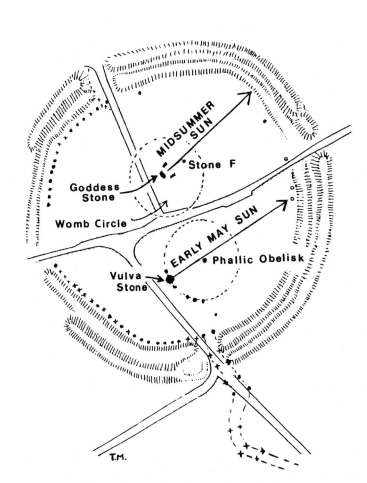

The major sunrise alignments at Avebury.
(1) The Vulva Stone of the southern circle is aligned on sunrise for the Spring Fertility Festival at the start of May. The rays of the sun achieve union with the Divine Vulva until replaced, for a few minutes, by the phallic shade of The Obelisk. Only at this time of the year and at the beginning of August (First Fruits Festival) does the shadow of The Obelisk meet the vulva of the Vulva Stone.
(2) The cove within the northern circle is orientated on sunrise for the Midsummer Fertility Festival. The rising sun pairs with the stone of the Great Goddess until eclipsed by the phallic tip of Stone F whose shadow meets the lower part of the waiting Goddess. As at Stonehenge, it was only at midsummer that this spectacle was possible: the arrangement had been carefully planned.

At the centre of the megalithic ring was a massive circular-based stone 6.5 metres, or 21 feet, high. William Stukeley asserted it to be the tallest stone at Avebury. The locals called it The Obelisk. Every year at the May Day Festival the rising sun shone past The Obelisk, and impregnated with light and energy an overtly-feminine image on what is unmistakably a Goddess-Vulva Stone. Once again we encounter the touching, dramatic spectacle of the Marriage of the Gods.

A few minutes later, as at the coves at midsummer and midwinter and similarly at Stonehenge in midsummer, the shadow of The Obelisk fused with the Goddess's vulva. This conspicuous mark, fully a metre long, is the most naturalistic rendering of a vulva known for prehistoric Britain; it is more explicit than the well-known Luffang vulva in Brittany. Visitors should make an effort to see it before 10 o'clock in the morning in the light of the sun. On Alexander Keiller's numbering system the megalith is simply Stone 106. In the spiritual world of the Neolithic Age the stone was the Goddess, who waited, fifty metres from the phallic Obelisk in a direction 63 degrees east of north, for sunrise on the morning of the Spring Fertility Festival.

Paul Devereux too has commented on the prominent vulva mark on Stone 106. In his book *Symbolic Landscapes* he provides a photograph, and remarks that the stone 'contains forms strikingly evocative of vulvar symbolism'.

This precision arrangement speaks volumes for the intentions of the planners and the exactness of the Sacred Marriage alignment, as at Stonehenge. It also informs us of the ancientness of May Day celebrations which, by 2500–2000 BC when Avebury's male and female stones were being arranged in their mating positions, must already have been a popular, much-loved event.

12

The Marriage Cult

The building of the great temples at Avebury and Stonehenge stemmed from the material and spiritual needs and immortal aspirations of anxious, pious peoples who were moved to stage-set their mythical imagery in a sensational scenario. Raised in dependable, timeless stone, the temples were intended to last for ever. Now that the hostility suffered by the Avebury megaliths in recent centuries has ended, and despite the lesser but unremitting attacks of the weather, the immutability and might of the remaining megaliths and the care of an enlightened society should guarantee their safety.

We can now see how the principle of the midwinter, May Day and midsummer Weddings of the Goddess at Avebury, made visually splendrous at the two coves and The Obelisk, was anteceded by the mating principles inherent in the long-barrow traditions of the region.

The earliest long barrows, as at Horslip (on the side of Windmill Hill) and South Street (near Beckhampton Cove), were largely or wholly earthen mounds. South Street long barrow, which is under the low hill close by to the south-east, was orientated at least approximately and probably intentionally on the midwinter sunrise. The rather later barrows of East Kennet and West Kennet had megalithic chambers, the former, like Stoney Littleton thirty kilometres to the west, awaiting midwinter sunrise, the latter the equinoctial sunrises.

The barrows intended for the winter hierogamy awaited the most southerly rising of the sun along the eastern horizon. On our Gregorian calendar this turns out to be on or close to 21 or 22 December which is the shortest day. Throughout all Neolithic and Bronze Age prehistory the midwinter celebrations would have been around 21–30 December which, by consequence of being the turning point for the sun, would have been thought of as New Year's Day. It was because this well-loved event in the European calendar could not be eradicated or displaced when the Christian missionaries arrived that they chose to celebrate Christ's birthday at this time as a convenient means of smothering its true origins.

The closure of the chambered long barrows in the Avebury region about the middle of the third millennium corresponded roughly with the debut of the Avebury stone circles and the rise of the coves. The still earlier earthen barrows may have served similar purposes as well, so a continuity of belief is discernible from the start of the fourth millennium to the end of the second millennium. A similarity of function would further emphasise that the ancient long barrows were not primarily built as tombs. They were Goddess shrines and their foremost purpose was as places of ritual and worship, with at certain times of the year celebration of the perennial theme of the Marriage of the Gods. In a region such as the Cotswold Hills, where there were dozens of fine chambered long barrows *but no stone circles*, we can see that it was the barrows which were the centre of attention on the great festival days, particularly the days when the Divine Marriage was welcomed and honoured.

To what extent was this rite built into Britain's other megalithic monuments? The extent of the cult was countrywide, and was revealed in different ways at various times and places during the three thousand years for which visible evidence is available in the form of surviving monuments. I think it likely that the rite was universally understood and adored—in Neolithic Europe too—and was practised by communities everywhere, even when no megalithic or other signs remain today.

There is at Stanton Drew, less than ten kilometres from the centre of Bristol in the west of Britain, a magnificent megalithic complex comprising three stone circles, a cove and other menhirs, which ranks third in England behind Avebury and Stonehenge. The theme of hierogamy seems to be suggested in the north-east circle. These stones consist of enormous blocks of silica-bearing brecchia (a rock of coarse composition), one of which, although now fallen, seemingly had the right azimuth for the sun at its midsummer rising to cast its broad shadow to the centre of the ring, where some sacred object or holy person might have been waiting. The arrangement could be deliberate, for the ground slopes strongly in the Stonehenge fashion but more markedly, which has the effect of shortening and strengthening the shadow. The circle once consisted of eight standing stones, but as five are now fallen we cannot be certain of its exact shape. The diameter is nevertheless 30–31 metres, close to the diameter of the first Stonehenge and the Durrington Walls timber circle.

From this circle a short avenue leads eastwards, more exactly on a bearing of 96

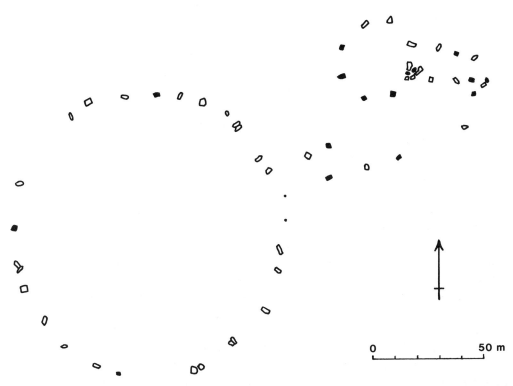

Circles and avenues at Stanton Drew south of Bristol towards the Mendip Hills. A third circle and the cove are off the map to the south-west. The stones are shown double size. The great circle has a diameter of 113 metres. *After L. V. Grinsell*

degrees from north. It is possible that this was formerly recognised as the alignment of the local equinox, but equinoctial bearings were not always evaluated well in prehistoric times because the sun was not at a turning point of its cycle. The great circle at Stanton Drew has an avenue too, with a middle bearing of 55° east of north, which approximates rather poorly with the local midsummer solstice, the hills to the northeast delaying the sunrise by a few degrees. A Sacred Marriage stone arrangement might have been intended within this structure, because when the sun is just above the horizon in this direction the long shadows of the avenue stones interlink with one another and join up. Similar ideas can be advanced for some other stone avenues, as at Callanish in the Outer Hebrides for the equinoxes (approximately). Added to the fine stone circle at Callanish at an obviously later date is an east-facing chambered cairn which is built within the small stone ring, also with a central pointed megalith. We must also allow for the fact that in some regions, before the advent of the mega-

The cove at Stanton Drew today. The Goddess Stone lies in pieces, the male stones misshapen but still erect on either side.

lithic period or where suitable stone was anyway lacking, sacred avenues were constructed using timber posts, but the position of very few have been recovered.

Surprisingly but significantly, the local name for the Stanton Drew circles is The Weddings, a name which could hark back to the Neolithic and Bronze Age Sacred Wedding. In 1723 William Stukeley recorded, 'The noble monument is vulgarly called the Weddings and they say 'tis a company that assisted at a nuptial solemnity thus petrified'. A folk story tells how the stone rings were once the guests at a wedding feast, who became petrified for dancing on the sabbath. This story sounds very like a Christianised rendering of a still more archaic original dating from the time when the Sacred Wedding festival was a major annual event in the region.

The cove at Stanton Drew is placed on a straight line with the centres of the great circle and the north-east circle but not in sight of either due to an intervening ridge. Stukeley was told that traditionally the three stones of the cove were known as the parson, bride and bridegroom. Could this be a deformed folk memory surviving from prehistoric times—that one of the stones was the 'bride', where Bride referred to the ancient Goddess and the main cove stone was her cult object? No evidence for a missing fourth stone has been recorded, nor does the cove face any sunrise position, but as Aubrey Burl points out, its direction approximates to the extreme southern moonrise. If it was a reunion with the moon that was intended, then a fourth stone (as at Avebury) would be dispensable, due to the weakness of the moon's shadow, and some other lunar device or rite invoked, as may have happened with the recumbent Goddess Stones at stone circles in Scotland.

At Arbor Low in Derbyshire a central cove faces the northern moonrise according to Aubrey Burl. Again, because of the feeble light of the moon, the shadow trick is ineffective and unnecessary. It sufficed that the Goddess Stones of these coves faced the desired moonrise, so that the Moon Goddess made contact nocturnally.

In Oxfordshire, at the stone circle known as the Rollright Stones, Divine Marriage may also have been practised, but the position is unclear because some of the stones have been damaged or moved. Their number has even increased in the last couple of centuries. There is certainly an entrance to the circle from the 'midwinter' south-east direction, and a stone of the circle seems to stand in the 'midsummer' position at the north-east.

Another interesting site is Mayburgh, at Eamont Bridge, near Penrith in Cumbria. The high bank of this magnificent henge is made of pebbles and stones from the nearest river bed and valley. An entrance in the east admits the rays of the rising sun at the spring and autumn equinoxes. At the centre of the henge a magnificent megalith stands, but missing are three near-neighbours which were to its north-east, east and south-east respectively as indicated on an old plan. It would be worthwhile to probe for the stone-holes in order to find their exact angles relative to what appears to be a very fine Goddess Stone. Not far away, on higher sloping ground near Little Salkeld, is the splendid megalithic circle known as Long Meg and her Daughters. Long Meg is a red sandstone outlier placed in line with the midwinter sunset as seen from the centre of the stone circles. Its long shadow would stretch right across the centre of the circle as the sun went down for the night.

Cairnpapple, on a hill-site between Edinburgh and Glasgow, was another ritual centre which had a cove. The great circle at Stenness in Orkney has a damaged cove which faced the magnificent Neolithic temple of Maeshowe. The nearby Ring of Brodgar may have boasted a cove, too, at what is now called the Comet Stone.

Many dozens of Goddess temples at which Sacred Marriage ceremonies took place can be identified across Britain, Ireland and France. Several based on megalithic architecture are listed in Table IV, chosen to give a representative selection from different parts of these countries. There are many more, besides non-megalithic barrows from all parts of Britain. These include the earthen barrows described in earlier chapters in connection with the Dorset Cursus and the Stonehenge Cursus. In some cases precise

The Goddess Stone in Mayburgh Henge with the eastern entrance beyond. Seven other megaliths which played their role in the scenario are missing.

measurement of alignments is not possible—but precision of orientation may not always have been thought necessary by the prehistoric worshippers. If the date of the solstice could be determined by some other means, such as the use of horizon identification markers, then the monument served its primary purpose as religious precinct and temple. Furthermore, the ceremony of the Marriage of the Gods might have been celebrated by some communities on other days of the year as well, especially Imbolc (1 February), May Day, Lammas (1 August), and Samhain (31 October), so that some monumental or megalithic alignments may denote these solar directions instead.

Above all else, the barrows, like the circles, were Goddess monuments. In Cheshire near Congleton, there is an east-facing chambered barrow with crescent-shaped forecourt called the Bridestones, the name probably a relic of the Goddess herself via the ancient British Goddess Bride whose name lives on as the Christianised St Bride. The two-part terminal chamber of the Bridestones is divided by a 'port-hole' slab, which

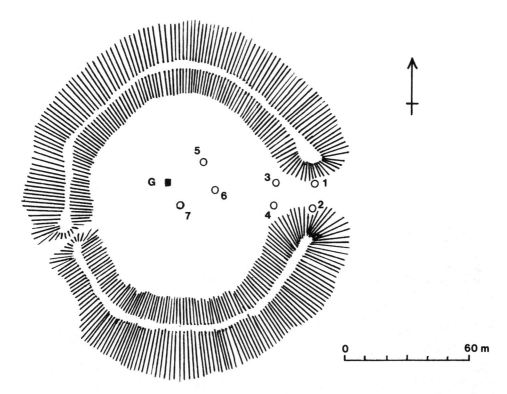

Map of Mayburgh Henge with stone positions according to Pennant. At the spring and autumnal equinoxes the sun shone through the vulvar gap between the entrance megaliths (stones 1–4) and consummated the Marriage with the Goddess Stone G which was completed by the phallic shadow of stone 6.

can be realistically interpreted as a cervix or womb-opening of the Goddess as at some of the Cotswold-Severn Goddess long barrows and Gallic chambered barrows. The Cotswold Hills have fine examples of chambered tomb-temples facing critical directions between north-east and south-east, many or most of which could have served their communities as places for performing Sacred Marriage rites on various dates of the year. These even include long barrows with so-called blind entrances, as at Belas Knap (although in this case the celestial alignments are with side cells rather than the axis). This restored barrow in Gloucestershire has a deeply-horned forecourt, inset with a *trilithon* façade and backstone which allows it to be interpreted as a cove-like arrangement of stones. The same may be said of many of Britain's cromlechs which have a horizontal megalith supported head-high by three or more huge standing stones, such as Kit's Coty (Kent), Lanyon Quoit (Cornwall), Pentre Ifan (Dyfed) and Bodowyr

TABLE IV

Some Goddess temples which seem to have been designed for Divine Marriage ceremonies

Name	County	Grid Reference	
Stonehenge	South Wilts	SU 123422	midsummer sunrise
Avebury, North Circle Cove	North Wilts	SU 103700	midsummer sunrise
Avebury, South Circle	North Wilts	SU 103698	May Day sunrise
Avebury, Beckhampton Cove	North Wilts	SU 089693	midwinter sunrise
East Kennet, barrow	North Wilts	SU 116669	midsummer sunrise
West Kennet, barrow	North Wilts	SU 105677	equinoctial sunrises
Stoney Littleton, barrow	North Somerset	ST 735572	midwinter sunrise
Stanton Drew stone circles	North Somerset	ST 601633	midsummer sunrise
Grey Mare and Colts, barrow	Dorset	SY 584871	midwinter sunrise
Hetty Pegler's Tump, barrow	Glos	SO 789000	midwinter sunrise
Nympsfield, barrow	Glos	SO 794013	midwinter sunrise
Randwick, barrow	Glos	ST 825069	midsummer sunrise
Hazelton South, barrow	Glos	SP 072188	midwinter sunrise
Heston Brake, barrow	Gwent	ST 505887	equinoctial sunrises
Addington, barrow	Kent	TQ 653592	midsummer sunrise
Kit's Coty, barrow/cromlech	Kent	TQ 745608	midwinter sunrise
Chestnuts, barrow	Kent	TQ 652592	equinoctial sunrises
Bridestones, barrow	Cheshire	SJ 906622	equinoctial sunrises
Bryn Celli Dhu, temple	Anglesey	SH 508702	midsummer sunrise
Swinside stone circle	Cumbria	SD 172883	midwinter sunrise
Mayburgh henge and stones	Cumbria	NY 519284	summer, winter, and equinoctial sunrises
Temple Wood stone circles	Argyll	NR 827979	midsummer sunrise
Newgrange, temple	Co. Meath	Ireland	midwinter sunrise
Newgrange, temple	Co. Meath	Ireland	midsummer sunrise
Newgrange, temple	Co. Meath	Ireland	midsummer sunset
Knowth, temple	Co. Meath	Ireland	equinoctial sunrises
Knowth, temple	Co. Meath	Ireland	equinoctial sunsets
Dowth, temple	Co. Meath	Ireland	midwinter sunrise
Gavrinis, Larmor-Baden	Morbihan	France	midwinter sunrise
Ty-ar-Boudiquet	Finistère	France	midwinter sunrise
Les Mousseaux, Pornic	Loire-Atlantique	France	midwinter sunrise

Dolmens and cromlechs, having a flat stone supported by vertical megaliths, present another aspect of Goddess imagery. While some may be the remains of earth-covered, galleried or single-celled long barrows, others were likely erected without any covering mound and may have changed little in the intervening years. This one is at Bodowyr, on the Isle of Anglesey, and has a typical womb-opening built to face the rising sun.

(Anglesey) among dozens of others. Some may be the remains of megalithic long barrows, as is commonly supposed, but some were perhaps raised, just as we see them today, as Goddess-worshipping temples with no surrounding mound of earth. Their symbolic representation of the Goddess's womb-opening reminds us once more of the latter's simple beginnings thousands of years earlier in the Palaeolithic era, and its subsequent development and ultimate realisation at Stonehenge as the most elaborate of all images to the Great Goddess.

13

The Goddess . . .
Then and Now

The solution to Stonehenge has been found, and with it a surprise, for it turns out that the monument, so long marvelled at for its mysteries and foreboding presence, has been storing a secret that concerns us all, one with a lesson for humankind.

We have seen how the peak of megalithic culture was reached by the building of ceremonial sanctuaries in which Heaven met Earth—centres which provided contact with the supreme divinities through manifestations materialising in timeless stone. The centrepiece of the ritual activity was the cult of the Great Goddess. In megalithic Britain and Ireland, as well as in Northern France, the Lady had always been known as a guardian divinity of the dead; now we have proof, revealed by the monuments themselves, that throughout the Neolithic Age her fecund powers were ascendant in the fields, in the animals, in women. At Stonehenge and at Avebury a remarkable ritual choreography was devised which united the heavenly powers of the Sun with the terrestrial dominion of the Goddess. The Cosmic Marriage had for a long time been a spiritual force. In a variety of forms it was celebrated everywhere that long barrows, henges, cursuses, circles and coves were built. By these sacred constructions monumental ceremonial reached the peak of its glory—and their supportive cultures lasted a further thousand years through much of the Bronze Age, before the warriors who built the Iron Age forts arrived with their importunate gods. Evidence of a celebration of Divine Marriage centred on a cult of the Goddess quickly diminishes after this, and wholly with the rise of Christianity, but in India and the Orient the archetypal Sacred Marriage continued and remains active to this day. The union of Indian Siva and Parvati, for example, was indeed another such wedding.

Throughout the prehistory of mankind primitive farming communities in all continents benefited from the reassurance and solace provided by mythologies inspired by the Marriage of the Gods. Recently recorded cases include tribal traditions from the North American continent where native Indians set down their beliefs in pictorial form—like the mating petroglyphs from California and Tennessee described in Chapter 10. As these dramatic concepts are merely the consequence of fundamental instincts deep in the psyche, their implications are open to psychoanalytical study, from which one finds that the Divine Marriage is an archetypal form at all levels of experience, one which ends in a fruitful, harmonious union. The marriage of Sun and Earth, or of Sun and Moon, is the unconscious symbolic joining of male and female principles which emanate from the psyche's congenital collective core. This is what makes the archetype so compelling and pervasive, why it so gloriously enriched the sacred symbolism of the Neolithic, why its sexual imagery appeals to free-thinkers so strongly today.

The truth and beauty of these revelations about Goddess religions is all too obvious to open-minded people, but in the western world the anti-sexual stance established so long ago within Judaeo-Christian traditions for a long time inhibited true understanding. By coupling attitudes of sin and shame to what is, after all, just normal sexuality, no understanding of the divine attributes formerly expressed by genital-organ idols is possible for these believers. They have no feeling for the divinity once thought to be localised in these organs, no appreciation that the latter represented for the old religions, as Barbara Walker so vividly put it, 'a part of the gods' paradise miraculously embedded in human flesh'. This contrasts with the situation of the Tantra-reading Hindu who is at ease with nature and the cosmic obligation of uniting the principles which *lingam* and *yoni* define. By symbolising the male and female organs in conjunction the Tantric altar stone depicts the essence of the origin of life, and unashamedly declares that Goddess and God perpetually conceive to maintain the universe as we know it.

The Egyptian *sma* or *sam* amulet radiated the same message, the *lingam* or penis in the *yoni* or vulva, while the mace—staff of office and symbol of authority known to the British Neolithic people with its beautifully carved and perforated bone or stone maceheads penetrated by a wooden shaft—originally bore the same significance, because its bearer owed his or her authority to the divine symbolism endowed in it by the principle of the Marriage of the Gods. This is not dissimilar from the orb and sceptre of today's regal authority, by which the spherical orb (standing for earth

The Divine Marriage, in which the personification of opposites, the Sun and the Moon, the Sky Father and the Earth Goddess, achieve sublime communion in an archetypal blend of the Male and Female principles. A seventeenth-century German engraving.

domination) held in the 'feminine' left hand, and the phallic sceptre held in the 'masculine' right hand, together symbolise the 'holy marriage' of monarch and country. In earlier times this Sacred Union was actually achieved by the wedding of the king with a priestess who personified the Goddess. As for the Yang and the Yin of the Chinese, Carl Jung declared that the intrinsic correspondence between the male and female principles—the complementary pairs of opposites called Yang and Yin—was substantiated philosophically by the ancient Chinese five thousand years ago; and he further noted that 'the oneness of man [sic] and the surrounding cosmos' displayed a deep regard of psychological fundamentals.

By celebrating the Marriage of the Gods the early societies were consciously blending archetypal images into a drama which typified their perennial fertility ambitions. Unconsciously, they were maintaining a coherent symbolic idea which arose in the psyche in primordial times, and is traceable back at least as far as 30000 BC, to the vulvar sculptures and art of the Upper Palaeolithic period with which this book began.

I am hopeful that it will prove beneficial for humankind that Stonehenge, so long admired as an unfathomable ruin from a former age, and which stands serene and lonely in a God-fearing country, has been re-identified as the peace-loving, benevolent Goddess—Herself an everlasting image of harmony and love. Having survived the dark ages of three thousand years since its abandonment as a working model of Goddess, Stonehenge may yet lead us back from a warring world and allow us to rediscover the social compatibility which should be achievable with balanced partnership societies.

In this monument we see a Holy Marriage whose consummation guarantees the fertility of the Earth. Its annual re-enaction reassures the community that the world is secure, and by demonstrating the unending cycle of life and continuance of the universe it maintains the everlasting immortality aspirations of the worshippers. The construction at Stonehenge is a working display and artistic statement of the life-generating union of sexual opposites which, by their conjunction, keeps the cosmic cycle in motion. Representing the whole Goddess in this drama, Stonehenge is an awe-inspiring tribute to Nature worship and love. For Goddess Worship is Nature Worship; and Goddess Love is Nature Love—the true and peaceful adoration of Earth and its mineral, vegetable and animal resources. Male-god worship imposes an unequal partition, arbitrarily enforced by male conquerors who have enjoyed thousands of years in a complacent and cruel suppression of half the world's population and who continually set at risk the entire world upon which we all depend.

The Goddess is alive because She is Mother Nature, She is Mother Earth. This is our birthright, the consequence of millions of years of evolution. Whether we are religious believers or not, Goddess *is* within us all through our love for and interdependence with Nature.

Brilliant Stonehenge. Love, Power, Equality, Security, Fertility, Immortality—this is your message, the celebration of Life itself.

Bibliography

This select bibliography lists useful works on archaeology, Goddess religions and symbology in which the reader can find additional details of the principal subjects treated in the text.

Stonehenge, Avebury and Their Times

ATKINSON, Richard J. C. (1979). *Stonehenge: Archaeology and interpretation*. Pelican, London (originally published by Hamish Hamilton, 1956).

BURL, Aubrey (1976). *The Stone Circles of the British Isles*. Yale University Press, New Haven and London.

BURL, Aubrey (1979). *Rings of Stone*. Frances Lincoln, London.

BURL, Aubrey (1979). *Prehistoric Avebury*. Yale University Press, New Haven and London.

BURL, Aubrey (1987). *The Stonehenge People*. Dent, London.

BURGESS, Colin (1980). *The Age of Stonehenge*. Dent, London.

CASTLEDEN, Rodney (1987). *The Stonehenge People*. Routledge & Kegan Paul, London.

CASTLEDEN, Rodney (1993). *The Making of Stonehenge*. Routledge & Kegan Paul, London.

CHIPPINDALE, Christopher (1983). *Stonehenge Complete*. Thames & Hudson, London.

CLARKE, D. V., COWIE, T. G. and FOXON, Andrew (1985). *Symbols of Power at the Time of Stonehenge*. HMSO, Edinburgh.

CLEAL, R. M. J., WALKER, K. E. and MONTAGUE, R. (1995). *Stonehenge in its Landscape*. English Heritage, London.

HEGGIE, Douglas C. (1981). *Megalithic Science*. Thames & Hudson, London.

MALONE, Caroline (1989). *Avebury*. Batsford, London.

RICHARDS, Julian (1990). *The Stonehenge Environs Project*. Historic Buildings and Monuments Commission, London.

RICHARDS, Julian (1991). *Stonehenge*. Batsford, London.

SMITH, Isobel F. (1965). *Windmill Hill and Avebury: Excavations by Alexander Keiller 1925–1939*. Oxford University Press, Oxford.

STUKELEY, William (1740). *Stonehenge*. London.

STUKELEY, William (1743). *Abury*. London.

UCKO, Peter J., HUNTER, Michael, CLARK, Alan J., and DAVID, Andrew (1991). *Avebury Reconsidered*. Unwin Hyman, London.

Goddess Religions, Comparative Religion and Prehistoric Symbolism

EISLER, Riane (1987). *The Chalice and the Blade*. Harper & Row, London.

ELIADE, Mircea (1958). *Patterns in Comparative Religion*. Sheed & Ward, London.

ELIADE, Mircea (1978). *A History of Religious Ideas: vol. 1. From the Stone Age to the Eleusinian Mysteries*. University of Chicago Press, Chicago.

EVASDAUGHTER, Susan (1996). *Crete Reclaimed*, Heart of Albion Press, Wymeswold, Loughborough.

GADON, Elinor W. (1989). *The Once and Future Goddess*. Harper & Row, San Francisco.

GIMBUTAS, Marija (1982). *The Goddesses and Gods of Old Europe: 6500–3500 BC Myths and Cult Images*. 2nd edn. Thames & Hudson, London.

GIMBUTAS, Marija (1989). *The Language of the Goddess*. Harper & Row, San Francisco. Thames & Hudson, London.

GIMBUTAS, Marija (1991). *The Civilisation of the Goddess*. Harper, San Francisco.

LERNER, Gerda. (1986). *The Creation of Patriarchy*. Oxford University Press, Oxford.

MEADEN, Terence (1991). *The Goddess of the Stones*. Souvenir Press, London.

NEUMANN, Erich (1963). *The Great Mother: An Analysis of the Archetype*. 2nd edn. Princeton University Press, New Jersey.

STRAFFON, Cheryl (1997). *The Earth Goddess*, Cassell, London.

WALKER, Barbara G. (1983). *The Woman's Encyclopedia of Myths and Secrets*. Harper & Row, San Francisco.

WALKER, Barbara G. (1988). *The Woman's Dictionary of Symbols and Sacred Objects*. Harper & Row, San Francisco.

OTHER REFERENCES

The works cited are listed under the first chapter to which they are appropriate although some appertain to more than one chapter.

Chapter 1. The Wonder of Stonehenge

EMERSON, Ralph Waldo. *The Problem*.

STEVENS, Edward T. (1882). *Jottings on Stonehenge*, p. 72. Brown and Co, Salisbury, England.

Chapter 2. The Universal Womb

BORD, Janet and Colin (1987). *Ancient Mysteries of Britain*, p. 238. Paladin, London.

CYRIAX, T. (1921). Ancient burial places. *Antiq J.*, vol. 28.

DAMES, Michael (1976). *The Silbury Treasure*, pp. 110–12. Thames & Hudson, London.

DE VRIES, Ad. (1974). *Dictionary of Symbols and Imagery*, pp. 182–3. North-Holland, London.

FARMER, J. S., and HEMLEY, H. E. (1966). *Dictionary of Slang*, vol. 1, p. xxxi.

GIMBUTAS, M. *The Language of the Goddess*, p. 223 (pillar crypts). Harper & Row, San Francisco. Thames & Hudson, London.

GRAHAM, H. *Eternal Eve*, quoted by I. Opie and M. Tatem in *The Dictionary of Superstitions*, p. 199. Oxford University Press.

MUNSCH, J. (1986) has recorded triangular pieces of flint from the Early Palaeolithic which have had breasts and vulvas sculpted on them by knapping (a photograph is reproduced by Marija Gimbutas in *The Language of the Goddess*, p. 237).

OPIE, Iona and TATEM, Moira (eds.) (1989). *A Dictionary of Superstitions*, p. 199. Oxford University Press, citing *Folklore*, vol. 86 with regard to Brahan Wood, near Dingwall, in Ross-shire, Scotland.

WALKER, Barbara G. (1988). *The Woman's Dictionary of Symbols and Sacred Objects*, pp. 313–14. Harper & Row, San Francisco.

Chapter 3. Womb, Tomb and Temple

DARVILL, T. C. (1982). *The Megalithic Tombs of the Cotswold/Severn Region*, p. 26. Vorda, Highworth, Wilts. (Summarises the radiocarbon dating evidence for the Cotswold-Severn chambered barrows.)

ELIADE, M. (1958). *Patterns in Comparative Religion*, p. 412. Sheed & Ward, London.

EOGAN, G. (1986). *Knowth*, p. 147. Thames & Hudson, London.

Chapter 4. The Marriage of the Gods

CAMPBELL, Joseph (1974). *The Mythic Image*, pp. 38–9. Princeton University Press, New Jersey.

CIRLOT, J. E. (1971). *A Dictionary of Symbols*, 2nd ed, p. 189. Routledge & Kegan Paul, London.

ELIADE, Mircea (1958). *Patterns in Comparative Religion*, pp. 411, 412.

GIMBUTAS, Marija (1989). *The Language of the Goddess*, p. 321.

GREEN, Miranda (1986). *The Gods of the Celts*, p. 73. Alan Sutton, Gloucester; Barnes and Noble, Totowa, New Jersey.

MARSCHAK, A. (1972). *Roots of Civilization*, pp. 320–21. McGraw Hill, New York.

MELLAART, James (1967). *Catal Hüyük: A Neolithic town in Anatolia*, plate 83 facing p. 149. McGraw Hill, New York.

WESTROPP, H. M. and WAKE, C. S. (1875). *Ancient Symbol Worship*, p. 26. 2nd ed., republished 1972. Curzon Press, London.

WOODWARD, P. J. (1988). Pictures of the Neolithic: Discoveries from the Flagstones House excavations, Dorchester, Dorset. *Antiquity*. vol. 62, pp. 266–74.

Chapter 5. The Sky God Mates with Earth

AESCHYLUS. Frag. 44, *Tragicorum Graecorum Fragmenta*, ed. Nauck, p. 44.

ASHBEE, P. (1984). *The Earthen Long Barrow*. 2nd ed., pp. xxxiii–iv.

ATKINSON, R. (1955). The Dorset Cursus. *Antiq. J.* 29, pp. 4–9.

BRADLEY, R. (1983). The bank barrows and related monuments of Dorset in the light of recent fieldwork. *Proc. Dorset Nat. Hist. Soc.*, vol. 105, pp. 15–20.

BRADLEY, R. (1986). *The Dorset Cursus: The Archaeology of the Enigmatic*, pp. 8, 16. Wessex Lecture III. Council for British Archaeology, Group 12, Salisbury.

BRADLEY, R., CLEAL, R., GARDINER, J., LEGGE, A., RAYMOND, F., and THOMAS, J. (1984). Sample excavation on the Dorset Cursus 1984. *Proc. Dorset Nat. Hist. and Archaeol. Soc.*, vol. 106, pp. 128–32.

BURL, A. (1987). *The Stonehenge People*, pp. 94, 115.

CHRISTIE, P. (1963). The Stonehenge Cursus. *Wilts Arch Mag*, vol. 58, pp. 370–83.

CIRLOT, J. E. (1971). *A Dictionary of Symbols*, p. 315.

CORNWALL, I. W. (1953). *Proc. Prehistoric Soc.*, Vol. 19 pt. 2, pp. 129–47.

CRAWFORD, O. G. S. (1957). *The Eye Goddess*. Phoenix, London. (Refers to *Sumer 1*, plates III, IV.)

Current Archaeology (1969). No. 1, pp. 2–4.

CURWEN, E. C. (1929). Excavations in The Trundle, Goodwood, 1928. *Sussex Arch. Collections*, vol. 70, p. 32 ff.

DYMOND, D. P. (1966). Ritual monuments at Rudston, East Yorkshire, England. *Proc. Prehistoric Soc.*, 32, pp. 86–95.

ELIADE, M. (1958). *Patterns in Comparative Religion*, p. 76 ff, 99, 259.

ELIADE, M. (1969). *Images and Symbols*, p. 41. Sheed & Ward, New York.

FRAZER, J. G. (1922). *The Golden Bough, A*

Study in Myth and Religion, Ch. 15, abridged version.

HOARE, R. C. (1812). *Ancient Wiltshire*, vol. i, p. 65. Inside the long barrow Warminster 1 'at the south end was a sarsen stone five feet high, terminating almost in a point, and placed in an upright position'. Somewhat similarly a large conical sarsen once stood at the south side of the entrance to the Wor Barrow enclosure.

LOVEDAY, R. (1985). *Cursuses and Related Monuments of Great Britain*. Unpublished Ph.D. thesis, Leicester University.

MEADEN, G. T. (1985). *Tornadoes in Britain*, p. 91. Commissioned Report for H.M. Nuclear Installations Inspectorate, Bootle, Lancs. (Available from their library; Bodleian, Oxford; and National Meteorological Library, Bracknell.)

NEWMAN, Paul (1987). *Gods and Graven Images*, Robert Hale, London.

NORTH, John (1996). *Stonehenge*, HarperCollins, London.

O'CONNELL, M. (1986). The Heathrow/Stanwell Cursus. *Current Arch.* Vol. 9, no. 99, pp. 122–5. Tornado tracks can be long and narrow like this narrow cursus (width 20 metres); a recent narrow-path tornado track was the Grantham to Newark one of 8 October 1977. Observer reports suggested a width of 15–20 metres (see *J. Meteorology*, vol. 3, pp. 35–9, 40–2, and 143, 1978).

PENNY, A. and WOOD, J. E. (1973). The Dorset Cursus complex: a Neolithic astronomical observatory? *Arch. J.*, vol. 130, pp. 44–76.

RICHARDS, J. (1984) in R. Bradley and J. Gardiner, *Brit. Archaeol. Report* no. 133, pp. 177–87. See also photograph in *Beyond Stonehenge*. 6. Trust for Wessex Archaeology, Salisbury (1985).

SMITH, A. C. (1860). *Wilts. Arch. Mag.* vol. 6, pp. 365–89.

STARTIN, D. W. A. (1982). Prehistoric Earthmoving, pp. 153–6, in H. J. Case and A. W. R. Whittle, *Settlement Patterns in the Oxford Region*. Research Report 44, Council for British Archaeology, Ashmolean Museum, Oxford.

STONE, J. F. S. (1947). The Stonehenge Cursus and its Affinities. *Antiq. J.*, vol. 104, pp. 7–19.

THOMAS, N. (1955). The Thornborough Circles, near Ripon, North Riding. *Yorkshire Arch. J.* vol. 38, pp. 425–45.

VIRGIL. *The Aeneid*. Book 4, pp. 165–6.

WAINWRIGHT, G. J. (1979). *Mount Pleasant Excavations 1970–71*, pp. 167–68. Thames & Hudson, London.

Wiltshire Arch. Mag., vol. 46, p. 320, 1933, and vol. 47, p. 76, 1935.

Chapter 6. The Stonehenge Cursuses

ASHBEE, P. (1984). *The Earthen Long Barrow*, p. 158.

BURL, A. (1987). *The Stonehenge People*, pp. 18 (Fig. 3), 19–20, 30, 62, 162.

HAWLEY, W. (1926). Report on the excavations at Stonehenge during the season of 1926. *Antiq. J.*, vol. 6, p. 4 (cf Burl A., *The Stonehenge People*, p. 97).

HOARE, R. C. (1810). *Ancient Wiltshire*, Vol. i, pp. 117, 157, 158. 'We next observed a rude conical pile of large flints, inbedded in a kind of mortar made of the marly chalk dug near the spot. This rude pile was not more than four or five feet in the base, and about two feet high on the highest part, and was raised upon a floor, on which had been an intense fire, so as to make it red like brick.'

MEADEN, G. T., and BROWN, P. (1979). *J. Meteorology*, U.K. vol. 4, pp. 201–2.

ORTIZ, Fernando (1947). *El Huracan*, Mexico City.

RICHARDS, J. (1984) in *British Archaeol. Report* no. 133, pp. 177–87.

ROBERTSON-MACKAY, M. E. (1980). A head and hooves burial beneath a round barrow on Hemp Knoll, near Avebury, Wiltshire. *Proc. Prehistoric Soc.*, vol. 40, pp. 123–176.

STONE, J. F. S. (1947). The Stonehenge

Cursus and its affinities. *Arch J.*, vol. 104, pp. 7–19.

THURNAM, J. (1869). On ancient British barrows, Part 1. Long barrows. *Archaeologia*, vol. 42, pp. 161–244, 182.

Chapter 7. The Henge of Stonehenge is Born

BURL, A. (1987). *The Stonehenge People*, pp. 62, 64–5.

Chapter 8. The Marvel of the Stonehenge Alignment

ATKINSON, R. J. C. (1978). Some new measurements on Stonehenge. *Nature*, vol. 275, pp. 50–2.

AUBREY, John (1980–2). *Monumenta Britannica*, vol. 1, p. 93. Sherborne, Dorset.

BURL, A. (1987). *The Stonehenge People*, pp. 57, 78–9.

ELIADE, M. *The Quest: History and Meaning of Religion*, p. 33. Chicago and London.

PETRIE, W. M. F. (1880). *Stonehenge: Plans, Descriptions and Theories*. London.

WOOD, J. E. (1978). *Sun, Moon and Standing Stones*, p. 163. Oxford University Press.

Chapter 9. The Marriage is Consummated

GIMBUTAS, M. (1982). *The Goddesses and Gods of Old Europe*, pp. 227–30 (dates the Sacred Marriage concept in S. E. Europe back to 6500 BC at least).

Chapter 10. Goddesses of Stone

AUBREY, John (1982). *Monumenta Britannica*, vol. 1, p. 74.

BAKKER, J. A. (1979). Lucas de Heere's Stonehenge. *Antiquity*, vol. 53, pp. 107–11, and plates 9 and 10.

BROME, James (1707). *Travels over England*.

BURL, A. (1985). *Megalithic Brittany*, p. 77.

BURL, A. (1992). Review. *Antiquity*, vol. 66, pp. 987–8.

BURL, A. (1987). *The Stonehenge People*, pp. 138, 186–7, 220.

BURL, A. (1994). Stonehenge: Slaughter, Sacrifice and Sunshine. *Wiltshire Arch. Mag.*, vol. 87, pp. 85–95

CASTLEDEN, R. (1987). *The Stonehenge People*, p. 111; also R. J. C. Atkinson (1956) in *Stonehenge* (p. 77), on the need to remove the bluestones to some place of safety.

HAWKINS, G. S., and WHITE, J. B. (1966). *Stonehenge Decoded*, p. 82. Fontana/Collins.

HAWLEY, W. (1922). Second report on the excavations of Stonehenge. *Antiq. J.*, vol. 2, p. 50.

HAWLEY, W. (1924). Fourth report on the excavations at Stonehenge. *Antiq. J.*, vol. 4, pp. 30–9 (pp. 31, 37).

HAWLEY, W. (1925). Report on the excavations at Stonehenge during the season of 1923. *Antiq. J.*, vol. 5, pp. 20–50.

KEELER, Clyde (1978). Tree of life and labyrinth. *Occasional publications of the Epigraphic Society*, Arlington, Mass., vol. 5, part 2, article 107, pp. 27, 28.

PITTS, M. W. (1979). On the road to Stonehenge: Report on the investigations besides the A344—1968, 1979 and 1980. *Proc. Prehistoric Soc.*, vol. 48, pp. 75–132.

Chapter 11. The Goddess at Avebury

CAMPBELL, J. (1973). *The Masks of God. Primitive Mythology.* 2nd ed., pp. 24, 437. Souvenir Press, London.

DEVEREUX, Paul (1992). *Symbolic Landscapes*, p. 152. Gothic Image, Glastonbury.

GRAY, H. St.G. (1934). The Avebury excavations, 1908–22. *Archaeologia*, vol. 84, pp. 99–162. (Browne's painting faces p. 101, there is a note on p. 108.)

SMITH, Isobel (1965). *Windmill Hill and Avebury*, p. 205, Fig. 70.

STUKELEY, W. (1743). *Abury*, pp. 23, 24.

Chapter 12. The Marriage Cult

GRINSELL, L. V. (1977). *Stanton Drew Stone Circles* (7pp. pamphlet). HMSO, London.

THE BUILDING OF A NEW STONE CIRCLE

With the coming of the third millennium it is proposed to raise a major stone circle on the downs of Britain, a circle that will endure forever. The monument has been designed with elegance and spirituality in mind, and with the aspiration that the entire nation will be involved through the finding and transport of megaliths from different parts of Britain. A replica of Stonehenge is not envisaged but there will be design and functional similarities. The preliminary plan incorporates alignments embracing all eight festivals of the solar year and the eight limiting azimuths of the 18.6-year lunar cycle.

Like Stonehenge which has seen four and a half millennia go by, the new monument is to be an impressive, everlasting construction which should soon establish an appeal and mystique of its own. Bearing in mind that it is, above all, a temple, it will differ from Stonehenge in being permanently open to the public who will have unrestricted access to the centre.

Interested parties should approach either Terence Meaden at 54 Frome Road, Bradford-on-Avon, Wiltshire BA15 1LD, or Gary Mann at 9 Grove House, 95 Addison Road, Holland Park, London W14 8DB.

Index

CP refers to the colour plates; pictures in the text are indicated by page numbers in italics.